India's Composite Heritage

{334}

India's Composite Heritage
A Workbook for Children and Parents

Nachiket Chanchani

ALEPH

ALEPH

ALEPH BOOK COMPANY
An independent publishing firm
promoted by Rupa Publications India

First published in India in 2022
by Aleph Book Company
7/16 Ansari Road, Daryaganj
New Delhi 110 002
Copyright © Nachiket Chanchani 2022

All rights reserved.

The author has asserted his moral rights.

Publication of this book is made possible by a grant from the
History of Art Department at the University of Michigan, Ann Arbor.

The views and opinions expressed in this book are those of the author and
the facts are as reported by him, which have been verified to the extent
possible, and the publisher is not in any way liable for the same.

The publisher has used its best endeavours to ensure that URLs for external
websites referred to in this book are correct and active at the time of going to
press. However, the publisher has no responsibility for the websites and can
make no guarantee that a site will remain live or that the content is or will
remain appropriate.

No part of this publication may be reproduced, transmitted, or stored in
a retrieval system, in any form or by any means, without permission in
writing from Aleph Book Company.

ISBN: 978-93-93852-43-4

1 3 5 7 9 10 8 6 4 2

Printed in India.

This book is sold subject to the condition that it shall not, by way of trade
or otherwise, be lent, resold, hired out, or otherwise circulated without the
publisher's prior consent in any form of binding or cover other than that in
which it is published.

Contents

	Introduction	1
	How to Use This Book	2
	Rock Shelters at Bhimbetka	4
	Dholavira at Khadir	8
	Great Stupa at Sanchi	12
	Mahabodhi Temple Complex at Bodh Gaya	18
	Caves at Ajanta	24
	Caves at Elephanta	30
	Caves at Ellora	36
	Mahavihara at Nalanda	42
	Monuments at Mahabalipuram	48
	Monuments at Pattadakal	54
	Temples at Khajuraho	60
	Rani-Ki-Vav at Patan	66
	Great Living Chola Temples at Tamil Nadu	72
	Rudreshwara Temple at Palampet	78
	Qutub Minar Complex at Delhi	80
	Archaeological Park at Champaner-Pavagadh	86
	Sun Temple at Konark	92
	Monuments at Hampi	98
	Historic City of Ahmedabad	104
	Hill Forts of Rajasthan	108
	The Fort at Agra	114
	Tomb of Humayun in Delhi	118
	Monuments at Fatehpur Sikri	122
	The Red Fort at Delhi	128
	Taj Mahal at Agra	134
	Churches and Convents of Goa	140
	Jaipur City in Rajasthan	144
	Jantar Mantar at Jaipur	150
	Victorian Gothic and Art Deco at Mumbai	154
	Chhatrapati Shivaji Terminus at Mumbai	158
	Le Corbusier's Capitol Complex at Chandigarh	162

Author: Nachiket Chanchani
Editor: Swati Chanchani
Editorial Assistant: Shweta Venkatesh
Design: Anirban Dutta Gupta
Illustrations: Namrata Toraskar and Anirban Dutta Gupta
Additional Illustrations: Grishma Verma

Introduction

India is home to many visual languages. A visual language is a means of communicating using elements and principles of art. The elements of art include line, shape, form, value, space, colour, and texture; and the principles of art include rhythm, balance, contrast, proportion, gradation, harmony, variety, and moment. Artists and architects communicate with the viewer by organizing the elements and principles of art in a thoughtful and attractive manner.

Innumerable works of art and architecture have been made in India over the ages. Of these, thirty-two monumental architectural complexes scattered in far corners of our country are particularly important because many meanings and diverse messages are compressed into their forms.

In addition, the thirty-two monumental architectural complexes in this book serve as milestones in the history of India, from prehistory to the present. Besides acquiring visual literacy, you will come to appreciate India's composite heritage that is made up of many parts. Finally, you will learn how to study history. History is a process of investigation and a way of knowing the past rather than a collection of facts. Historians identify and use diverse types of evidence to construct a narrative. Historians also strive to situate a particular event or process within a wider context. Our hope is that you will be able to begin this endeavour by the time you finish reading this book and complete all its activities.

How to Use This Book

The name of the monument and the location are graphically treated with 'texture' inspired from the place.

The main illustration of the monument may also have an activity related to it.

This text gives an introduction to the specific monument.

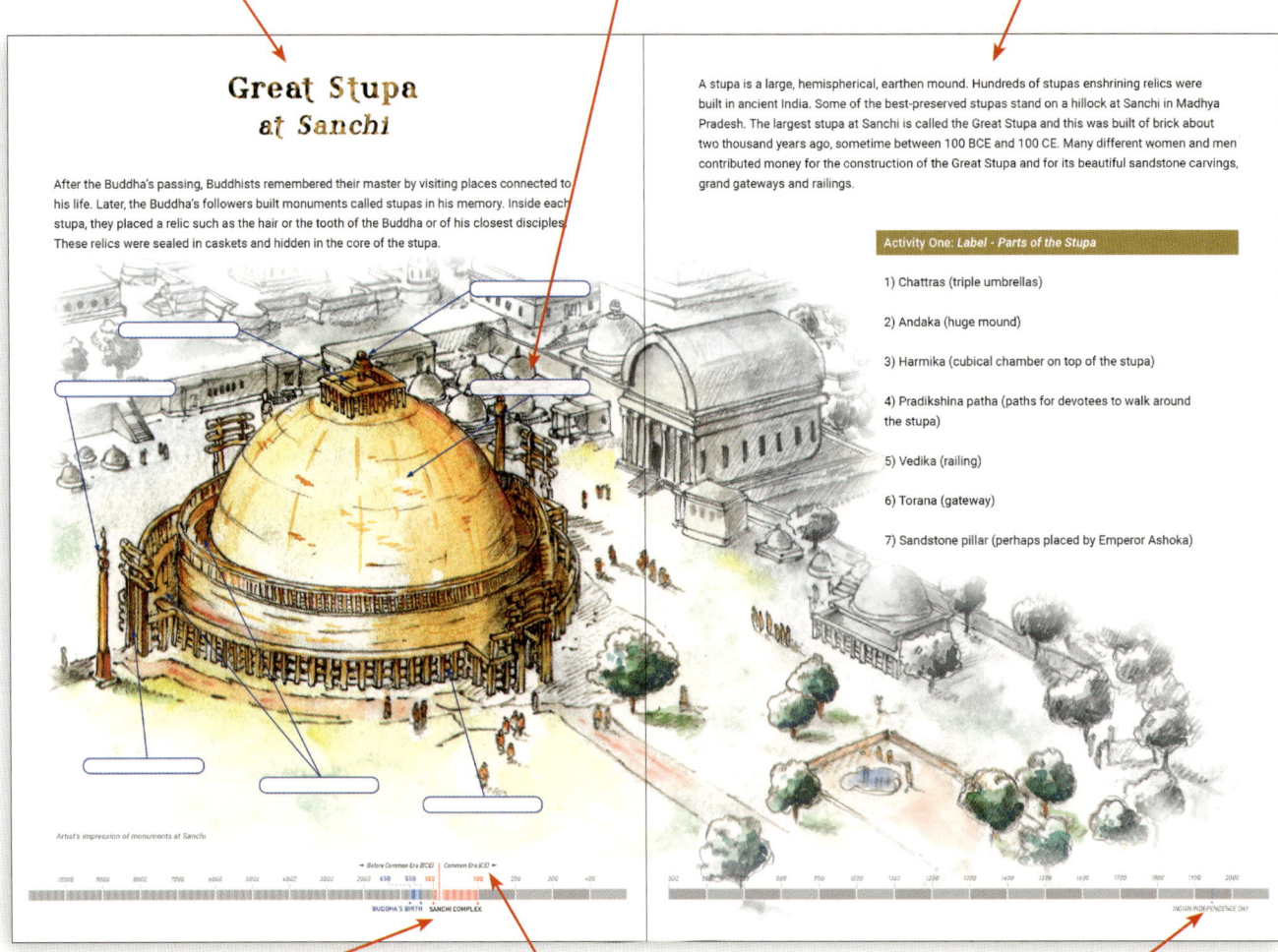

A timeline at the bottom indicates the time period when the monument was constructed. It is shown in bands of dark and light pink.

Additional information may also be indicated using bands of dark and light blue.

The timeline is divided into two segments—BCE or Before Common Era and CE or Common Era.

To give a sense of scale, 1947, the year of India's independence, is indicated on the timeline.

Each monument is identified by a distinct colour code. The activity number and description are also written on this coloured band.

A common activity is 'Point to' the map.

In certain cases additional information and instructions are given. Information is always written in regular font while instructions are written in *italic font (like this)*.

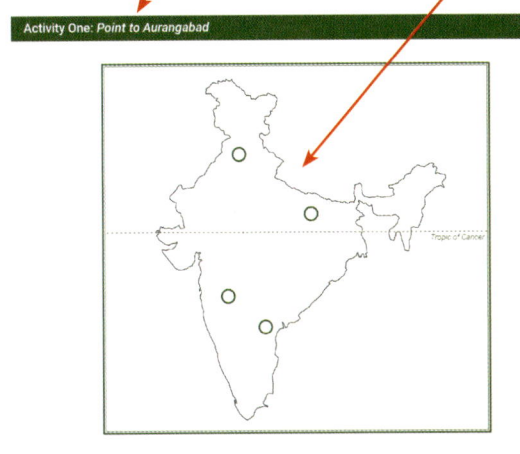

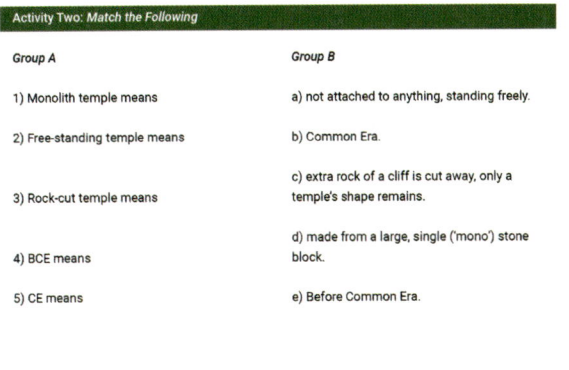

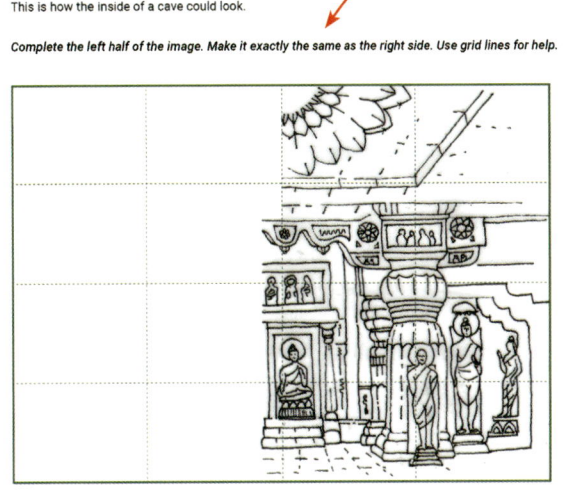

The pages are numbered at the bottom.

Some of the activities are partially completed and the participant is expected to complete the rest.

Rock Shelters at Bhimbetka

Very long ago people lived in caves, and sometimes they would draw on the walls of their caves. Today, their drawings are called cave art or rock art. They drew tigers, deer, wild boar, dogs, birds, crocodiles, lizards, and snakes. They also drew men hunting with bows and arrows, or riding horses and fighting with spears and swords, or riding on an elephant. Furthermore, they drew men and women: eating, cooking, drinking, playing, and dancing. They coloured their drawings red, yellow, green, black, and white. Sometimes, careless people drew on top of another person's drawings.

The cave art at Bhimbetka was done 'Before the Common Era' (look at the timeline). In fact, some of this art was done in approximately 8000 BCE, that is, a long time ago when people probably did not read or write, and did not practise farming. Instead, they ate roots and fruits that they gathered and animals that they hunted.

About 750 ancient cave homes, also called 'rock shelters', were discovered by an archaeologist in the wooded Bhimbetka hills near Bhopal. All of these caves do not contain rock art. However, a few caves in the hill that are hidden inside a forest called the Ratapani Wildlife Sanctuary, contain these ancient drawings and paintings.

INDIAN INDEPENDENCE DAY

Activity One: *Point to Bhimbetka*

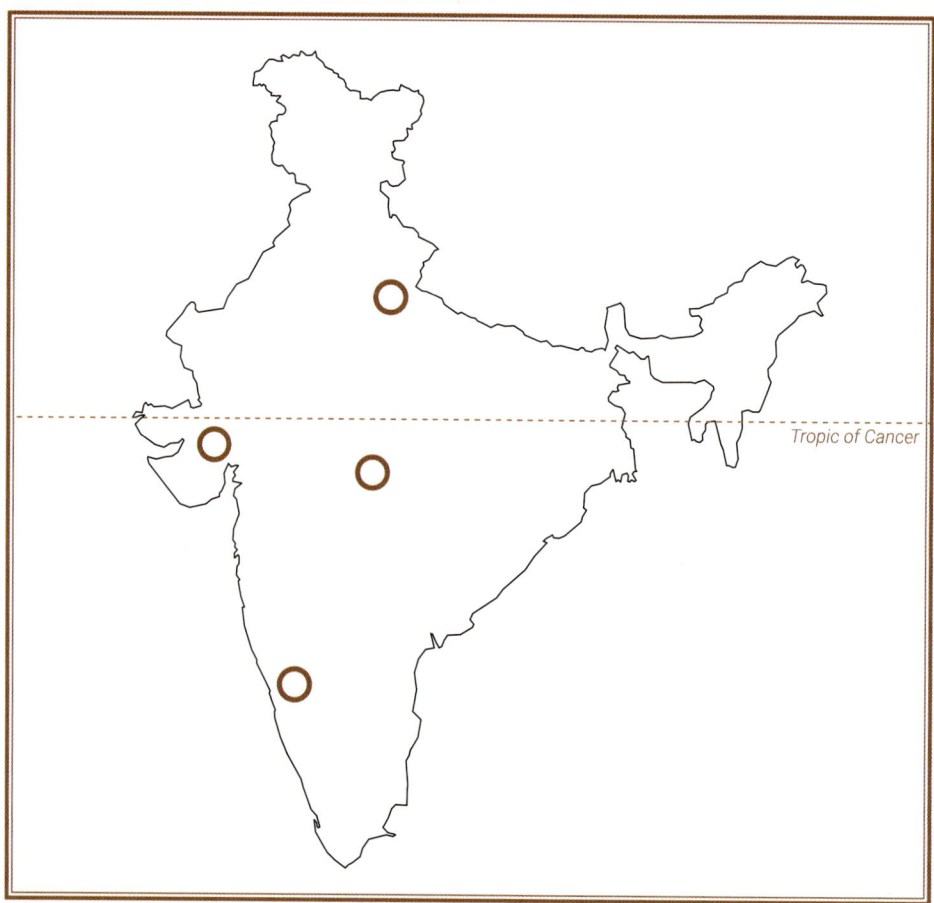

Activity Two: *Multiple Choice*

1) A person who unearths and identifies artefacts from the past is called an:
    a) archaeologist
    b) dentist
    c) musician

2) In cave art only a few colours are used:
    a) because the artists were lazy people.
    b) because the artists were colour blind.
    c) because only a few colours could be made from local plants and rocks.

3) In prehistoric times people **did not**:
    a) read, write, and farm.
    b) cook, sing, and dance.
    c) hunt, draw, and colour.

Activity Three: *Identify the Creatures on 'Zoo Rock'*

Point to the **Elephant, Deer, Buffalo** *and the* **Tiger-like** *creature!*

◯　　　◯　　　◯　　　◯　　　◯

Activity Four: *Colour the Timeline*

1) 8000 BCE to 5000 BCE (Blue)

2) 5000 BCE to 0 (Green)

3) 0 to 1000 CE (Orange)

4) 1000 CE to 2000 CE (Purple)

5) Mark the current year (Red)

Dholavira at Khadir

Humans have been on this planet for a long time. First they lived in caves: hunting, gathering, drawing. Later, humans began to farm and to store their surplus food. They started to write and record life around them, to trade with people far and near, and began living settled lives in urban clusters. Human history begins with the discovery of a few such clusters or civilizations. The Indus Valley Civilization is one of these; and the ruins of an ancient city at Dholavira are a part of this civilization.

The uniqueness of cities of the Indus Valley is that they were planned with broad, paved streets, with sanitation and drainage systems, and with homes built of standard-sized burnt clay bricks.

In addition to this, the people at Dholavira in the Rann of Kutch built underground reservoirs for collecting and storing rainwater; for this they drilled into solid rock using primitive tools. Moreover, they mined agate-carnelian, jasper, copper, limestone, and shell from the desert at Khadir. They made objects using these and traded them. Indeed, they were clever. The Indus people also had a script which nobody in the world has been able to decipher till now!

It is believed that Dholavira was closer to the sea than it is nowadays. Over the years, the landscape and the climate changed and the inhabitants of Dholavira gradually abandoned the city.

Activity One: *Point to Dholavira and the Indus River*

Activity Two: *Identify and Match—Objects from Dholavira*

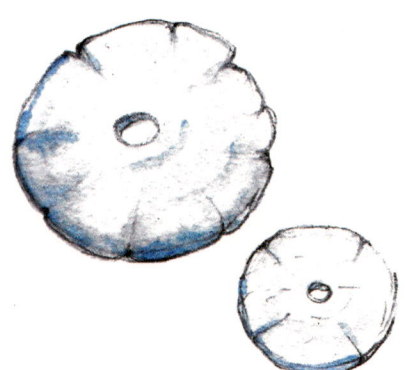

1) Arrowheads

2) Items made of shell

3) Script of the Indus Valley Civilization

4) Weights

5) Beads

6) Seals

7) Buttons

Activity Three: *Colour and Answer—Reconstructing a Broken Pot*

Archaeologists spent considerable time sticking together scattered pieces of this big broken pot.

Find a few missing pieces:

1) Look at all the numbered pieces and colour them in shades of brown. Remember that this is a curved pot and one side will be darker than the other side because of the way the surface reflects the light that falls on it. Colour them keeping that in mind. Use the numbers for guidance.

2) Look at the fragments on the right, and tick the ones which could be the missing pieces of the jar.

Dark Brown · Brown · Light Brown

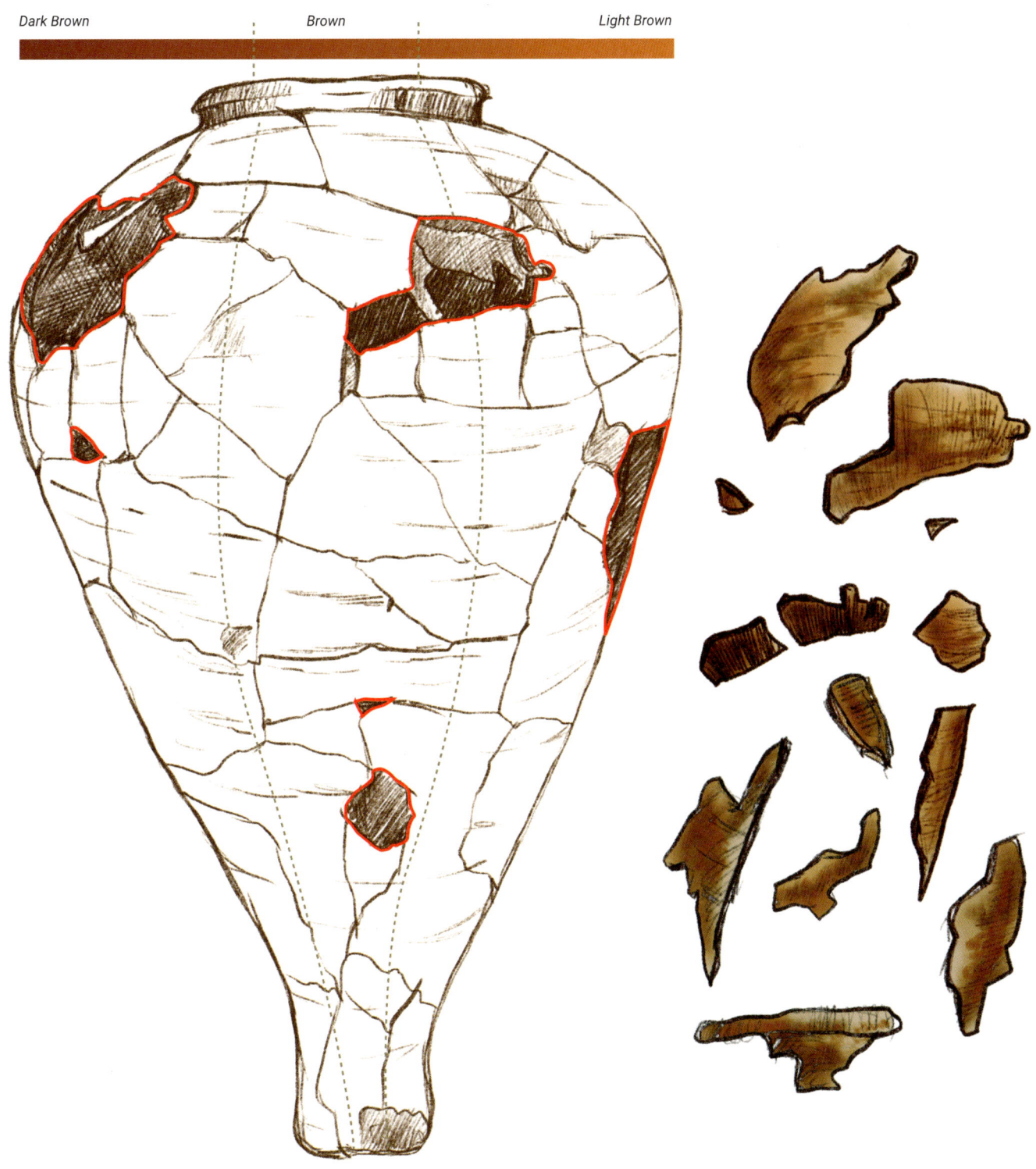

Great Stupa at Sanchi

After the Buddha's passing, Buddhists remembered their master by visiting places connected to his life. Later, the Buddha's followers built monuments called stupas in his memory. Inside each stupa, they placed a relic such as the hair or the tooth of the Buddha or of his closest disciples. These relics were sealed in caskets and hidden in the core of the stupa.

Artist's impression of monuments at Sanchi

A stupa is a large, hemispherical, earthen mound. Numerous stupas enshrining relics were built in ancient India. Some of the best-preserved stupas stand on a hillock at Sanchi in Madhya Pradesh. The largest stupa at Sanchi is called the Great Stupa and this was built of brick about 2,000 years ago, sometime between 100 BCE and 100 CE. Many women and men contributed money for the construction of the Great Stupa and for its beautiful sandstone carvings, grand gateways, and railings.

Activity One: *Label—Parts of the Stupa*

1) Chattras (triple umbrellas)

2) Andaka (huge mound)

3) Harmika (cubical chamber on top of the stupa)

4) Pradakshina patha (paths for devotees to walk around the stupa)

5) Vedika (railing)

6) Torana (gateway)

7) Sandstone pillar (perhaps placed by Emperor Ashoka)

Activity Two: *Point to Sanchi*

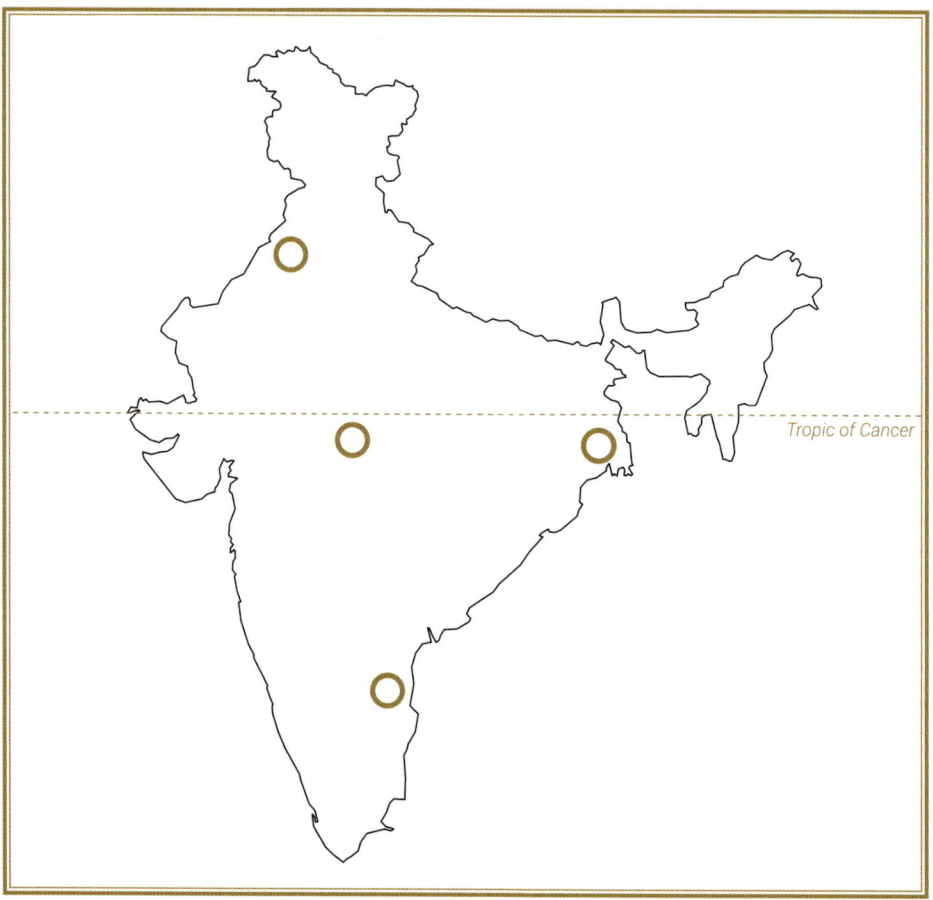

Activity Three: *Multiple Choice*

1) Approximately when did the historical Buddha live? (Look at the timeline.)
    a) In 2010, after the independence of India.
    b) In 900 CE, after the Great Stupa was built.
    c) In 650–500 BCE, before the Great Stupa was built.

2) A stupa is built to remember:
    a) Rani Lakshmibai of Jhansi
    b) Gautama Buddha
    c) Mahatma Gandhi

3) What is hidden deep inside a stupa?
    a) Relics such as a piece of bone or a lock of hair
    b) Biscuits
    c) Flowers

Activity Four: *Spot and Label*

This carving is of a gateway of the Great Stupa. It shows wild animals approaching the Bodhi (peepul) tree at Bodh Gaya under which the Buddha sat.

Spot and label the following animals: Eagle, Lion, Buffalo, Deer *and* Snake

Activity Five: *Match the Following*

Group A

1) Grand gateways are placed in four

2) Ashoka was a

3) The triple umbrella means that

4) Broad railings at Sanchi are made of

5) Pradakshina patha is a path used for

Group B

a) famous Buddhist king.

b) main directions: north, east, south, west.

c) devotionally walking around the stupa.

d) there is something important underneath.

e) sandstone and they are splendidly carved.

Activity Six: *Identify—Story of Mahakapi*

This sculpture shows a story from the *Jataka Tales*.

Identify the following five scenes in the story:

1) The Ganga River.
2) A troop of monkeys living in a grove on the right bank of the Ganga River.
3) Royal archer aiming his bow at the monkeys.
4) The monkey-king forming a bridge across the River Ganga to help his fellow monkeys cross.
5) The monkey-king teaching the human-king about royal duties.

Activity Seven: *Tick the Right Answers*

Which three buildings are inspired by the Sanchi Stupa?

Buddhist Temple
Luoyang, China

Garudastambha
Tiruvalla, Kerala

Plaza Cinema
Mumbai, Maharashtra

Somnath Temple
Veraval, Gujarat

Rashtrapati Bhavan
New Delhi, India

Meenakshi Temple
Madurai, Tamil Nadu

Rang Ghar
Sivasagar, Assam

Mahabodhi Temple Complex
at Bodh Gaya

Located in Bodh Gaya, Bihar, the Mahabodhi Temple Complex is a very important site for Buddhists. An offshoot of the original Bodhi tree, under which the Buddha became wise and enlightened, stands in the temple complex. Beneath this Bodhi tree is a seat called the Vajrasana, or more simply called the Diamond Throne, upon which the Buddha meditated more than 2,000 years ago. Pilgrims from Sri Lanka, Myanmar, Thailand, China, and other far-eastern countries have been visiting this site for hundreds of years and continue to do so.

Activity One: *Colour the Scene at the Bodhi Tree*

◄ Before Common Era (BCE) | Common Era (CE) ►

10000　9000　8000　7000　6000　5000　4000　3000　2000　1000　260　100　200　300　400

MAHABODHI TEMPLE COMPLEX

The Mahabodhi Temple was probably first made from wood and brick in approximately 260 BCE, and has been rebuilt many times since then. The main tower is very tall and there are four smaller towers around it. The statue of the Buddha inside the main temple is more than a thousand years old.

This complex, also called the Maha Vihara, contains seven sites that are especially sacred to Buddhists. They are related to the seven weeks that the Buddha spent in meditation after he received enlightenment. Apart from these, there are many small shrines and stupas.

Activity Two: *Pick the Right Answer*

1) A mudra is:
    a) a soft drink
    b) a hand position
    c) a song

2) Bhumisparsha mudra involves:
    a) raising the arms up to heaven in prayer
    b) folding the hands together in namaste
    c) a gesture where the fingers gently touch (sparsh) the earth (bhumi)

3) Inside the main shrine of the Mahabodhi Temple the Buddha is shown as:
    a) seated in the Bhumisparsha mudra
    b) watering plants
    c) driving a car

4) Based on the above answers which illustration resembles the mudra shown by the Buddha inside the main shrine of the Mahabodhi Temple?

Activity Three: *Point to Bodh Gaya*

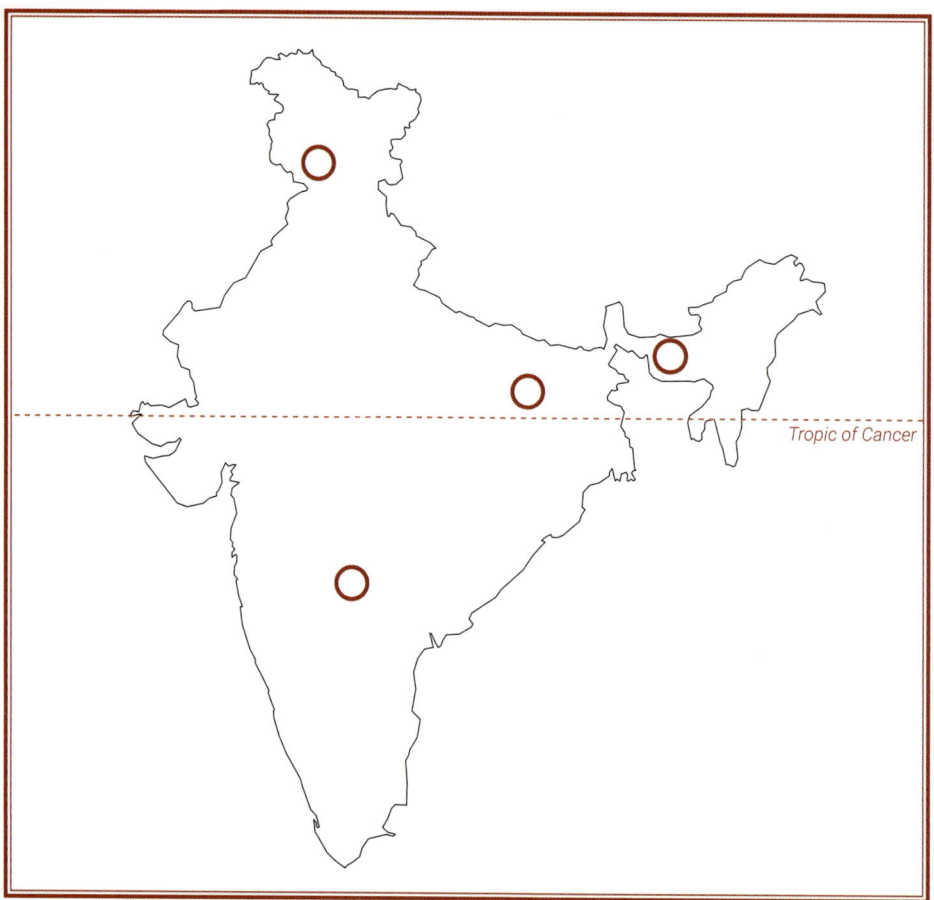

Tropic of Cancer

Activity Four: *Find the Words*

1) Mahabodhi

2) Bodh Gaya

3) Mahavihara

4) Buddha

5) Bodhi Tree

6) Buddhism

Y	Y	Y	Y	Y	Y	Y	Y	Y	Y	Y	B
J	M	A	H	A	B	O	D	H	I	J	O
J	A	J	J	J	J	J	J	J	J	J	D
X	H	X	X	X	X	X	X	X	X	X	H
Q	A	Q	B	U	D	D	H	A	Q	Q	G
Z	V	Z	Z	Z	Z	Z	Z	Z	Z	Z	A
K	I	K	K	K	K	K	K	K	K	K	Y
F	H	F	F	F	F	F	F	F	F	F	A
C	A	C	C	C	C	C	C	C	C	C	C
Y	R	Y	B	O	D	H	I	T	R	E	E
X	A	X	X	X	X	F	F	F	F	F	F
Y	Y	B	U	D	D	H	I	S	M	Y	Y

Activity Five: *Join the Dots and Answer*

This is a _____ (*bodhi leaf, coconut leaf, bamboo leaf*) which is also called a peepul leaf. This leaf is _____ (*rectangle-shaped, heart-shaped, square-shaped*) and is an important symbol in Buddhism.

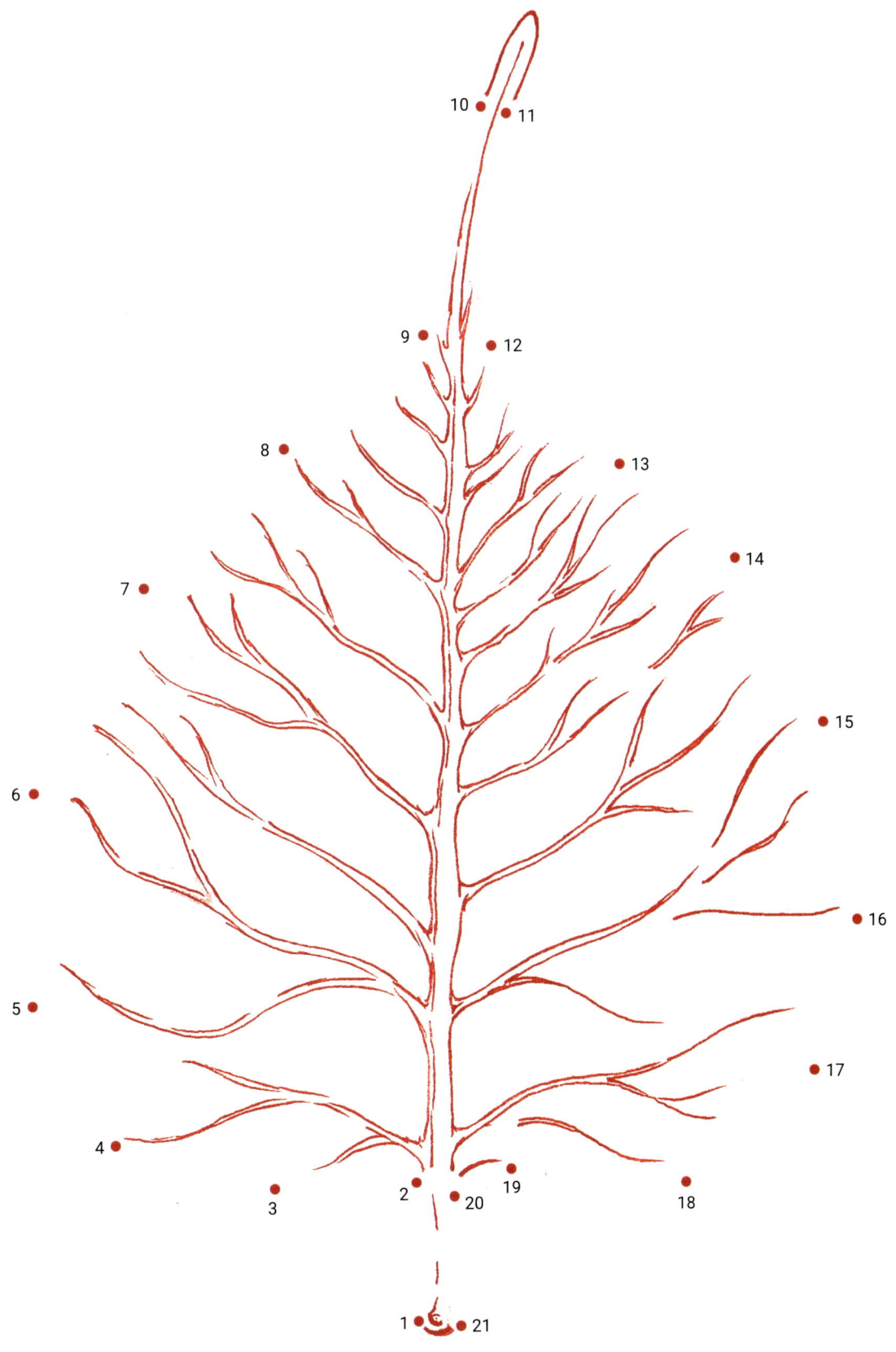

Activity Six: *Follow in the Footsteps of the Buddha*

There are seven sites in the temple complex important to Buddhists because the Buddha paused or passed by them. *Mark them on the site map given below.*

1) **The Bodhi Tree:** An offspring of the original Bodhi tree, also called the peepul tree, under which the Buddha obtained enlightenment.

2) **Animesh-lochan Chaitya:** The spot at which the Buddha sat and gazed at the Bodhi tree.

3) **Rajyatana Tree:** The Buddha paused here to give teachings.

4) **Ratnaghar Chaitya:** As the Buddha meditated here, six colours shone from his body.

5) **Ajapala Nigrodh Tree:** A banyan tree under which the Buddha meditated for a week.

6) **Mucalinda Sarovar:** The lake in which the serpent king Mucalinda lived.

7) **Ratna-chakrama:** A pathway between the Bodhi tree and the Animesh-lochan Chaitya that has carvings of lotuses.

Caves at Ajanta

Imagine cliffs, a wild, wooded gorge, and a river snaking along beneath. Here, a British officer was hunting for tigers but instead discovered many deep, dark caves. Several caves contained elaborate carvings and paintings.

In ancient times, Buddhist monks lived here. They chiselled out thirty caves on the steep face of a cliff made of hard basalt rock. The oldest cave was dug out about 2,200 years ago, and the newest about 1,500 years ago. These caves are near Aurangabad in Maharashtra.

◄ Before Common Era (BCE) | Common Era (CE) ►

10000 9000 8000 7000 6000 5000 4000 3000 2000 1000 150 | 100 200 300 400

AJANTA CAVES COMPLEX

Some caves contain stone beds—these were where monks slept; these residences of monks are called viharas. Other caves, where the monks gathered for meetings and prayers, are called chaityas. The chaityas have formal entrances decorated with stone sculptures and have pillars inside. Some even have a stupa within.

Certain caves have paintings; these are famous and well-loved. The ceilings have beautiful patterns, the walls show the story of the Buddha's life and also illustrate some *Jataka Tales*. The style of painting is special and called fresco.

Rulers and merchants supported the Buddhist monks who chose to live in this quiet and lovely space.

Activity One: *Point to Ajanta*

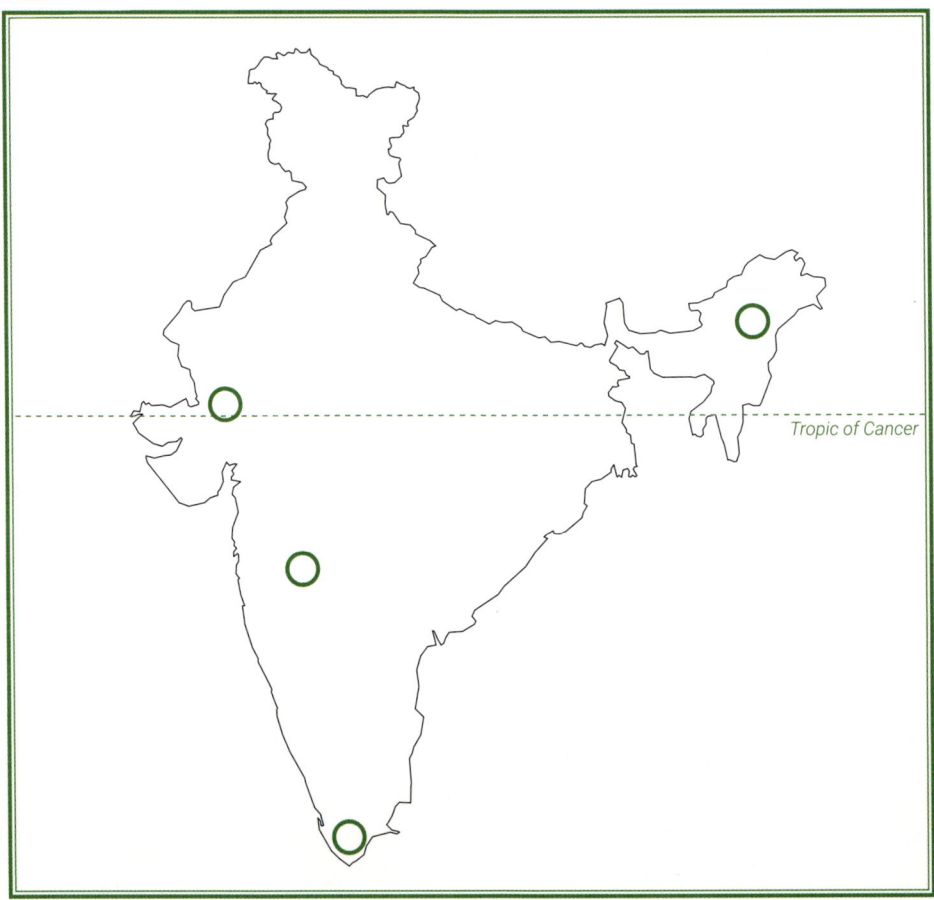

Activity Two: *Find the Words*

1) *(Basalt, Bamboo)* _____ is a type of igneous rock.

2) Igneous rocks are formed from lava flowing from _____ *(volcanoes, pine trees)*.

Activity Three: *Multiple Choice*

1) The colours of the paintings in Ajanta are bright even today because the caves were:
(dry, dimly lit, both).

2) The river that flows in the gorge below the Ajanta caves must be the:
(Nile, Ganga, Waghore).

3) Monks in Ajanta led simple lives studying, praying and also:
(painting, carving, both).

Activity Four: *Choose—Chaitya or Vihara*

1) This is the inside of:
A chaitya? A vihara?

2) This cave containing tiny bedrooms inside is called:
A chaitya? A vihara?

3) This is a grand entrance to:
A chaitya? A vihara?

Activity Five: Match the Following—Frescoes

Group A

1) Fresco means

2) Fresco paintings are done on walls

3) Paintings in Ajanta show scenes from

4) *Jataka Tales* are stories

Group B

a) the *Jataka Tales*.

b) about the prior lives of the Buddha.

c) while they are still wet.

d) fresh.

Activity Six: Match the Following—Colour to Source

Activity Seven: *Trace, Draw, Colour*

The ceilings of Ajanta have lovely patterns and are brightly painted.

Copy and join one pattern with another and create a complete Ajanta-type ceiling!

Caves at Elephanta

Temples are the homes of gods. However, in ancient times, more than 1,500 years ago, caves served as homes for gods. Caves on Elephanta Island, near Mumbai, serve as a home for the god Shiva.

Cave number 1 is famous and contains nine huge panels showing Shiva in different moods and often surrounded by other beings: attendants, musicians, other deities.

In one carving Shiva is shown as Natesha, the Lord of Dance; in another as a yogi. Yet another shows Shiva's marriage to Parvati. The most famous panel depicts Shiva as Trimurti—having three faces—one fierce, one dignified, one gentle.

Unfortunately, every panel at Elephanta has suffered damage. In some panels, an arm is missing or a head is missing. In others, the toes are missing or a nose is missing and so on. Sometimes, rough people purposely break sculptures. Damage to the sculptures also happens due to natural calamity, or due to some weakness in the structure.

There are several other ancient caves on this island. The cave walls, pillars, and sculptures are rough and black because they are composed of basalt rock. The roofs of the caves are held up by thick stone columns. The local name for this island is Gharapuri meaning the City of Caves.

When Portuguese travellers discovered this island, they noticed a big, stone elephant at the dock and therefore named it the 'Elephanta Island'. This stone elephant is now in a very broken condition and is placed at the entrance of the Mumbai Zoo.

Activity One: *Point to Elephanta and Explore the Island*

Find the nine places listed below and number the circles accordingly.

1) Jetty where one lands from Mumbai

2) Cluster of seven caves

3) Cannon Hill

4) Stupa 1

5) Stupa 2

6) Forest

7) Village

8) Stone Elephant found here near the Raj Bandar Jetty

9) Raj Bandar Jetty

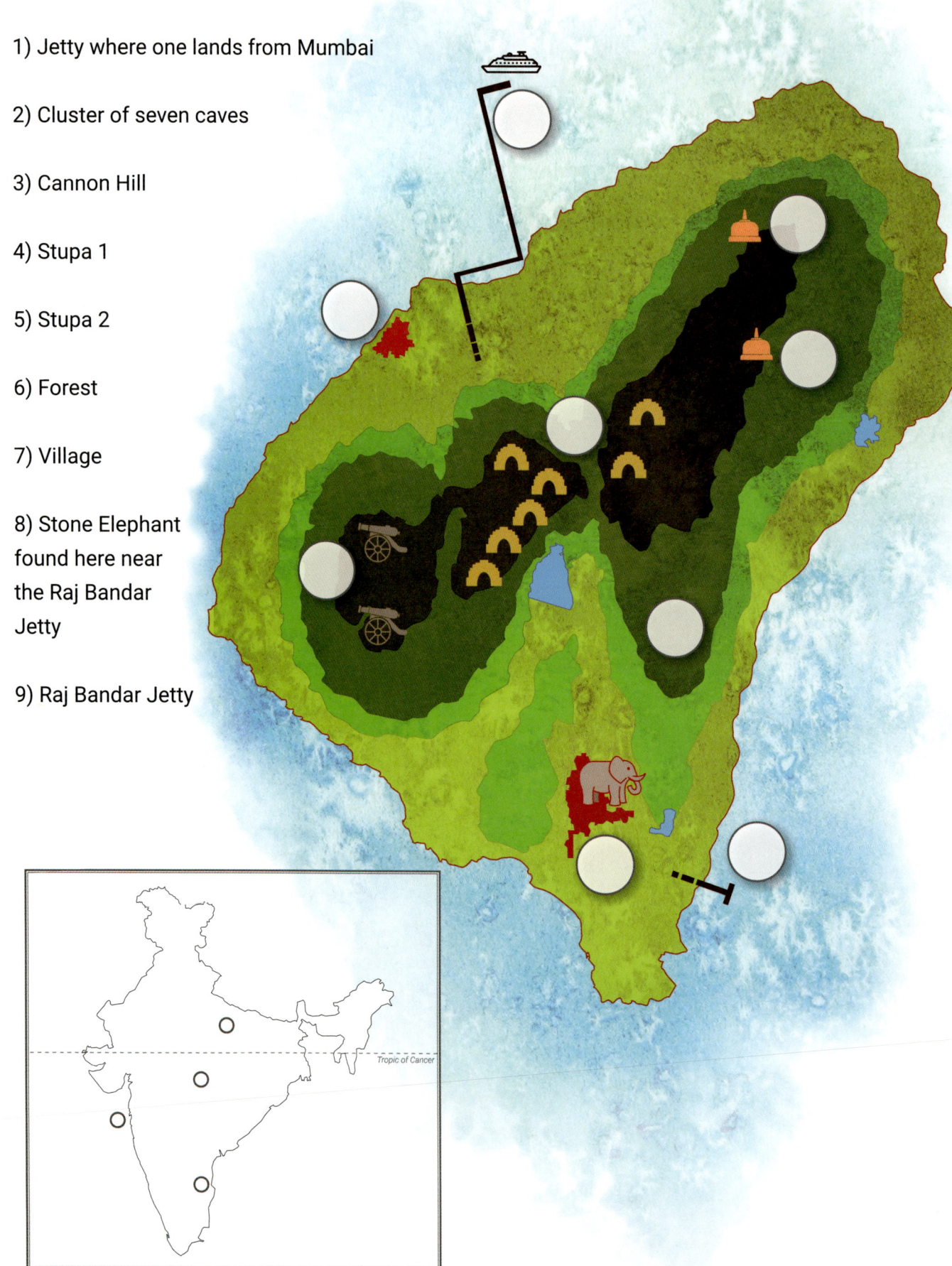

Activity Two: *Identify Details—Trimurti Panel*

Draw arrows from the circles and point out the following features. One element, broad shoulders, has already been done for you:

1) The Fierce, Masculine Face

a) moustache and thin lips

b) holding a poisonous snake

c) wearing a helmet

2) The Dignified, Peaceful Face

d) high royal crown and necklace

e) broad shoulders

f) eyes shut in meditation

3) The Gentle, Feminine Face

g) pouting lips, arched eyebrows

h) ringlets of hair surrounding the forehead

i) dainty decorations tucked into the hair

Activity Three: *Label Using Arrows—Natesha Panel*

1) Shiva, whose arms and legs are broken and is dancing.

2) Kartikeya, Shiva's elder son with a lance, watching his father's dance.

3) Ganesha, elephant-headed, standing beside Kartikeya, also watching his father.

4) Three-headed Brahma, god of creation, has come on a seat held up by swans.

5) Airavata, the elephant that bears Indra, king of the gods, has arrived.

6) Gandharvas, heavenly beings who can fly, have come to watch Shiva's dance.

Activity Four: *Point out—Kalayana Sundara Panel*

1) Shiva, coyly looking at Parvati.

2) Parvati, very shy, standing beside Shiva.

3) Himavat, standing behind Parvati, offering his daughter in marriage.

4) Attendant following Himavat, bringing a jar of water for the ritual.

5) Attendant following Parvati holding a fly-whisk.

6) Heavenly beings descending from the heavens to watch the marriage.

Caves at Ellora

At Ellora, there are caves upon caves—about one hundred of them stretching for two kilometres. These have been carved by human hands on the face of a long cliff. Some caves were used as resting places for pilgrims and monks, some as assembly and prayer halls, and yet others were mansions for gods.

Jain Cluster: *Small and large caves, assembly halls, free-standing shrines honouring Tirthankaras.*

Hindu Cluster: *Caves with carvings of stories about gods and goddesses, and free-standing, monolithic temples.*

◄ Before Common Era (BCE) | Common Era (CE) ►

10000 9000 8000 7000 6000 5000 4000 3000 2000 1000   100 200 300 400

These are not ordinary, forlorn caves—instead, they have ample natural light and are richly decorated. Many of the entrances and pillars have pleasing shapes and designs. On the inner walls, or on the outer walls, or on all walls of the caves—scenes from the lives of gods have been carved. The oldest caves have Jain motifs. Then there is a string of caves with Buddhist ideas, and then there is a large group of caves with Hindu narratives.

In some spots, the extra rock of the cliff was excavated away until the shape of a temple appeared. This is how the famous Kailashanatha Temple was made. There are special words to describe this style of making structures: rock-cut, free-standing, monolith.

Ellora caves are near Aurangabad in Maharashtra. The earliest caves were carved around 600 CE and the last ones around 1000 CE.

Buddhist Cluster: *Assembly halls, living spaces, and chapels for monks, nuns, and laypeople.*

ELLORA TEMPLE COMPLEX

INDIAN INDEPENDENCE DAY

Activity One: *Point to Aurangabad*

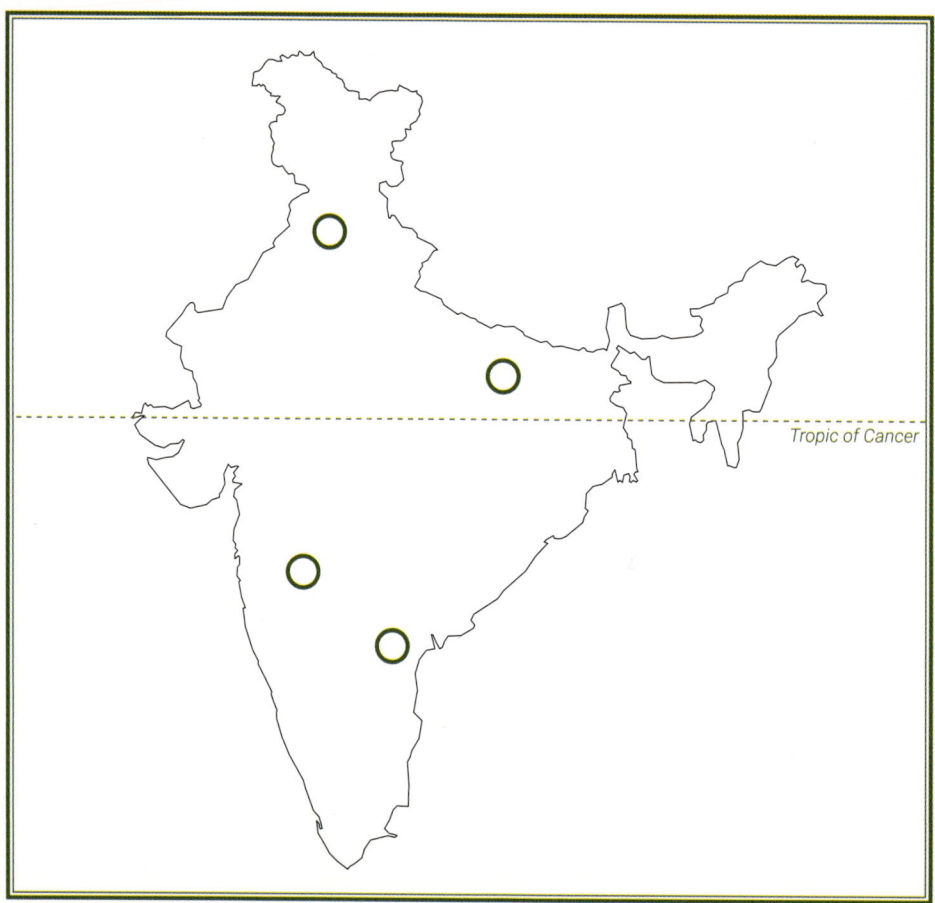

Activity Two: *Match the Following*

Group A

1) Monolith temple means

2) Free-standing temple means

3) Rock-cut temple means

4) BCE means

5) CE means

Group B

a) not attached to anything, standing freely.

b) Common Era.

c) extra rock of a cliff is cut away, only a temple's shape remains.

d) made from a large, single ('mono') stone block.

e) Before Common Era.

Activity Three: *Draw a Mirror Image*

This is how the inside of a cave could look.

Complete the left half of the image. Make it exactly the same as the right side. Use grid lines for help.

Activity Four: *Fill in the Blanks*

1) The caves at Ellora, Ajanta, and Elephanta are all _____ (*man-made caves, natural caves*).

2) A prayer room is also called a _____ (*chapel, kitchen*).

3) A small temple is called a _____ (*shrine, shrike*).

4) The long cliff at Ellora is formed from volcanic rock called _____ (*basalt, brick*).

5) The caves at Ellora have motifs that are Hindu, Jain, and _____ (*Buddhist, Christian*).

Activity Five: *Right or Wrong*

Which of these tools do you think the ancient stone carvers carried in their bags to carve the Ellora caves?

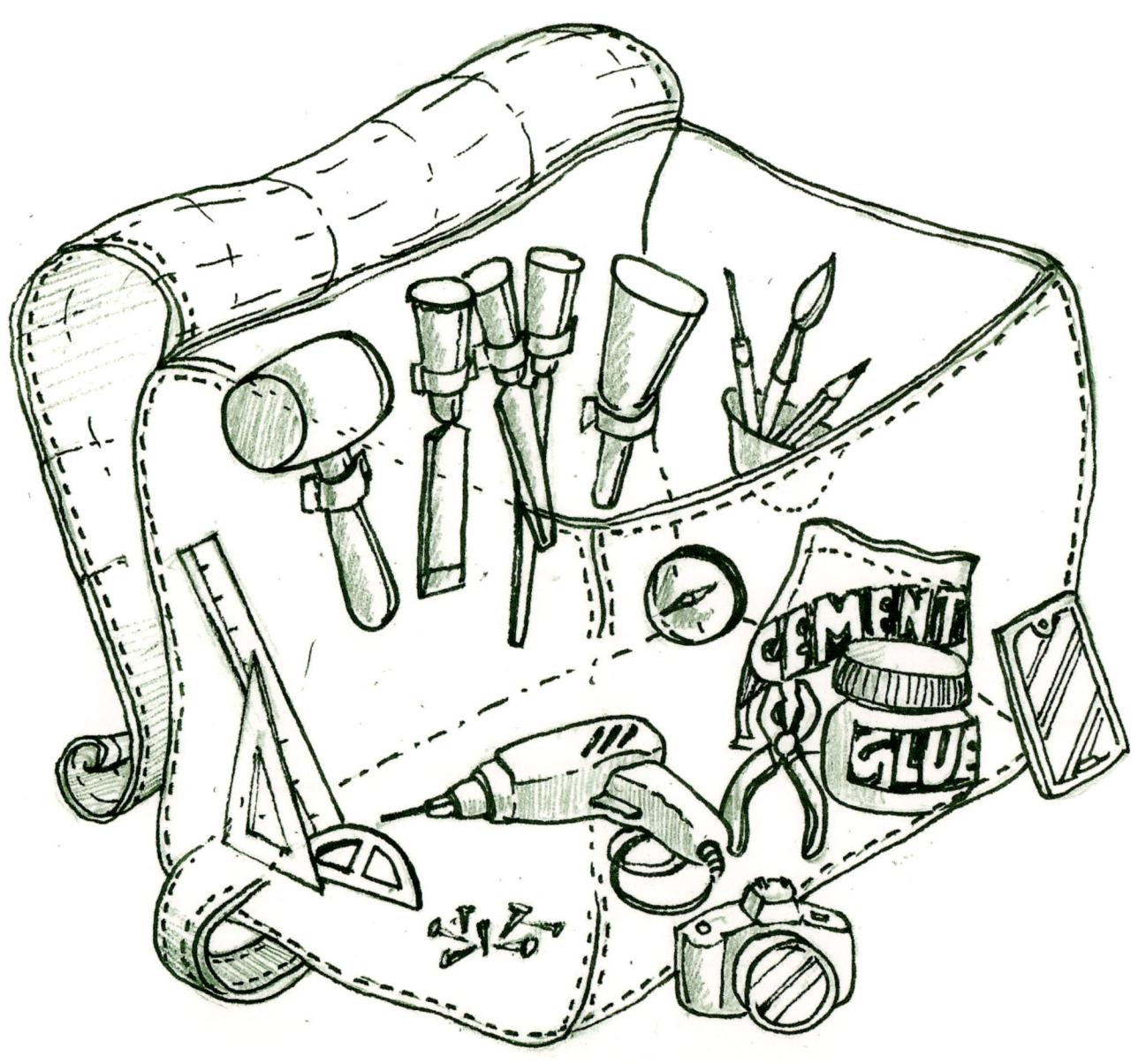

Activity Six: *Multiple Choice*

1) Those who are not monks and nuns are called (laypeople, old people, lazy people).

2) Buddhists call prayer halls and assembly halls (chaityas, vajras, stupas).

3) (Viharas, hotels, palaces) are spaces where Buddhist monks rested.

Activity Seven: *Yes or No*

Compare and contrast the two sculptures.

Siddharatha Gautama Buddha

Vardhaman Mahavira

1) Both are sitting on lion platforms, emblems of their royal lineages. [Y / N]

2) Both are flanked by attendants. [Y / N]

3) Both are reading books. [Y / N]

4) Both are sitting under trees. [Y / N]

5) Both are wearing clothes. [Y / N]

6) Both are in a hurry to go somewhere. [Y / N]

7) Both are seated in meditation in siddha asana. [Y / N]

8) Both are sitting on a lotus flower. [Y / N]

Mahavihara at Nalanda

Nalanda is the name of a place in Bihar, and Mahavihara refers to a campus such as a boarding school where many people live together and study. Virtuous Buddhist monks, young and old, lived here. Some were famous teachers; and visitors came from far and near to learn from them.

Rulers of this region, too, were impressed with this group of people and gave them money; tall buildings, temples, assembly halls, classrooms, and lotus ponds were built.

All this happened about 1,000 to 2,000 years ago. In fact, it took hundreds of years for the Nalanda Mahavihara to become a famous school. Then, gradually it became less popular; and finally, it was totally destroyed by aggressive people and thereafter forgotten.

Recently, the story of Nalanda became known from objects found in this place such as stone statues, metal coins, mud bricks, and also from what Chinese visitors wrote long ago in their diaries and from manuscripts. The exact dates of old objects are found by a procedure called carbon dating.

Activity One: *Point to Nalanda*

Activity Two: *Guess the Right Answers*

1) The following three were visitors who went from China to the Nalanda Mahavihara:
(*Xuanzang, Yijing, Sunil, Faxian*)

2) Students came from the following three countries to study at the Mahavihara:
(*Tibet, Canada, China, Korea*)

3) Three well-known teachers at the Mahavihara were:
(*Peter, Dignaga, Dharmakirti, Padmasambhava*)

4) The kings who helped the Mahavihara belonged to the following three empires:
(*Pala empire, Gupta empire, Egyptian empire, Gauda empire*)

5) Three subjects that students studied at the Mahavihara were:
(*Buddhist holy texts, Astronomy, Medicine, Computers*)

6) The following three types of remains were found at the Mahavihara:
(*Metal coins, Bamboo baskets, Stone sculptures, Clay pottery*)

7) The residents of the nearby villages provided the monks with these three items:
(*Ketchup, Milk, Rice, Butter*)

8) The dates of old objects can be known by these three methods:
(*Carbon dating, Seriation, Stratigraphy, Playing hockey*)

Activity Three: *Match the Following*

Group A	Group B
1) Manuscripts are always	a) mostly in olden times.
2) Manuscripts were created	b) the Prajnaparamita manuscript.
3) Manuscripts were written on material such as	c) handwritten.
4) Manuscripts remain well preserved in	d) cloth, palm leaf, bark, and leather.
5) A name of a manuscript regularly copied in Nalanda is:	e) dry climate.

Activity Four: *Label—Items found in Nalanda*

1) Small metal stupa

2) Clay keepsake with the Buddha in a teaching position

3) Round clay seal

4) Metal statue of the Buddha in the Bhumisparsha mudra

Activity Five: *Multiple Choice*

1) The Prajnaparamita manuscript is written in:
(*Arabic, Sanskrit, Spanish*)

2) The shape of a manuscript written on a palm leaf is:
(*slim and long, round, square*)

Activity Six: *Number the Scenes of the Buddha's life on the Prajnaparamita Palm Leaf Manuscript*

1) Birth of the Buddha from Queen Maya's side as she uses the branch of a tree and a companion for support.

2) The Goddess Prajnaparamita flanked by two lotuses in her hands, and surrounded by four disciples.

3) The Buddha meditating while four people, sent by Mara the demon, try to distract him.

4) A monkey giving the Buddha a bowl of honey.

5) The Green Goddess holding a single lotus in her hand, and flanked by two disciples.

6) The moment of the Buddha's passing away, and achieving nirvana.

Monuments at Mahabalipuram

The waves of the sea almost touch the monuments at Mahabalipuram, an ancient sea port on the shores of the Bay of Bengal in Tamil Nadu. The Shore Temple made of granite is the monument closest to the sea.

A little distance away, there are five unique temples commonly called Pancha Rathas. Astonishingly, each of these temples is carved from a single granite boulder, and each temple resembles a different kind of building, such as: a hut, a mansion, a meeting hall. Notably, some of these temples have a large, stone animal placed just outside.

This animal is the vahana of the god who is inside the temple. A vahana is the vehicle or the mount upon which the god can sit and ride. Also, at Mahabalipuram there are many caves that have been transformed into palaces and temples for gods.

The best-loved monument at Mahabalipuram is a huge, carved rock that shows the story of the River Ganga coming down from heaven to earth, while sage Bhagiratha prays nearby. However, some believe that the sculpture narrates another story—of Arjuna performing penance in the Himalayas and receiving a magic weapon from Shiva. Additionally, there are many delightful carvings of animals on this rock.

Activity One: Point to Mahabalipuram

Activity Two: *Show—Features on the Rock-carving*

1) A man performing penance standing on one foot

2) Flying gods and goddesses

3) Four-armed Shiva rewarding a man for his penance

4) A river

5) Carvings of nagas (snakes): king and queen

6) A sage seated near a shrine

7) A herd of elephants going to the river

8) Deer

Activity Three: *Draw—Trade Routes*

Draw the trade routes from Java and from Sri Lanka upto Mahabalipuram.

Activity Four: *Match the Following*

Group A

1) The animals which are vahanas are

2) 'Arjuna's Penance' and 'The Descent of the Ganga'

3) The Pancha Rathas

4) The cave temples are also called

5) Inside the cave temples there are many

Group B

a) are both names of the same rock-relief.

b) have no wheels.

c) a lion, a bull, and an elephant.

d) pillars and carvings.

e) mandapas.

Activity Five: *Spot and Colour*

Many artefacts such as **Roman amphorae, Chinese coins,** and **bits of broken pottery** were discovered in the seabed off the coast of Mahabalipuram.

Spot these artefacts in the drawing, and colour them.

Activity Six: *Name Three Pancha Rathas*

1) Shala—a long, rectangular meeting hall

2) Kuta—a thatched cottage

3) Prasada—a multi-storeyed mansion

Monuments at Pattadakal

Pattadakal is a dazzling place. There is a neat cluster of temples made of red stone that stands out against the blue sky. The soil is also red, the surrounding cliffs are red, and the sparkling Mahaprabha River flows past.

Pattadakal was a special spot for the Chalukya dynasty whose kings and queens developed this site, and where they probably conducted their coronation ceremonies here. Here, they certainly expressed their love for art, architecture, and experimentation; the temples combine the North Indian and South Indian modes of architecture called Nagara and Dravida. Also, these are amongst the earliest free-standing temples in India, built during the seventh and eighth centuries when builders and patrons were still trying to settle upon good layouts for Hindu temples.

The Pattadakal cluster has ten major temples and many smaller structures. These are dedicated mostly to Shiva, some to Vishnu, few to Devi, and one is a Jain temple. The largest temples are the Virupaksha and the Papanath.

Delightful carvings of scenes from classics such as Ramayana, Mahabharata, and various Puranas can be recognized on the walls of the temples. Moreover, there are inscriptions etched on pillars that tell us about the history of the place.

Activity One: *Guess*

1) The temples at Pattadakal are made of
(*red sandstone, grey basalt, green schist*).

2) A coronation ceremony is conducted to
(*crown a new king, mourn a death, give a sports medal*).

3) Inside the Jain temple at Pattadakal, there is a statue of
(*Jina, the Buddha, Jesus Christ*).

4) Shiva, Vishnu, and Devi are worshipped by
(*Hindus, Buddhists, Muslims*).

5) Temple walls are covered with sculptures and thus the walls are
(*like story books, boring, wet*).

Activity Two: *Point to Pattadakal*

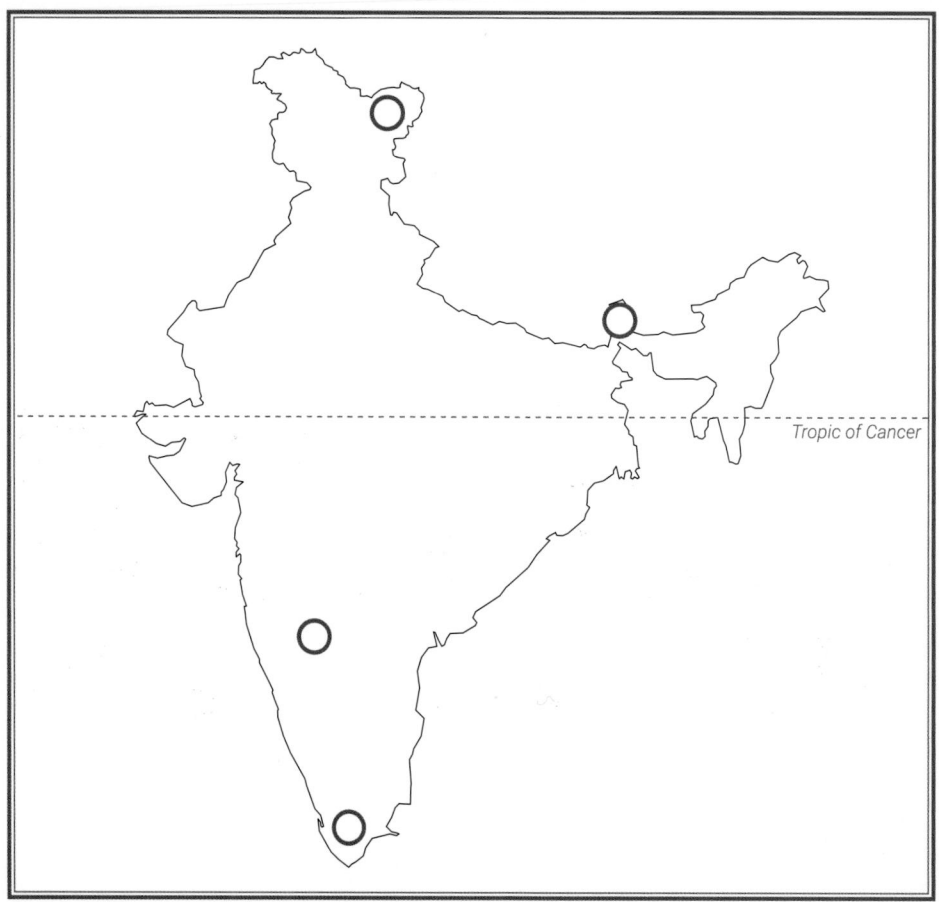

Activity Three: *Find the Names*

1) Chalukya

2) Mughal

3) Gupta

4) Chola

5) Pala

C	H	A	L	U	K	Y	A
X	X	X	X	X	X	X	X
M	U	G	H	A	L	W	W
F	F	F	W	W	Z	Z	Z
X	X	C	H	O	L	A	Z
X	G	U	P	T	A	W	Z
F	F	F	P	A	L	A	Z
F	X	F	X	X	Z	W	Z

Activity Four: *Colour—Modes of Indian Temple Architecture*

Dravida Mode

Nagara Mode

Activity Five: *Odd One Out*

1) Art, Architecture, Painting, Drawing, Swimming

2) Carved, Etched, Engraved, Jumped, Sculpted

3) Upanishads, Mahabharata, Tinkle, Ramayana, Puranas

Scene from the Mahabharata

Activity Six: *Composites 'Two-In-One'—What do you See?*

1)

a) An elephant
b) A bull
c) An elephant and a bull

2)

a) A swastika
b) Two cobras
c) Two cobras and a swastika

3)

a) Shiva
b) Parvati
c) Shiva and Parvati

Activity Seven: *Match the Following*

Group A

1) The study of inscriptions is called

2) Inscriptions tell us

3) Inscriptions are often written on

4) Inscriptions at Pattadakal are written

Group B

a) about the history of a place.

b) stone surfaces.

c) in various ancient Indian scripts.

d) epigraphy.

Inscription found at Pattadakal beside a sculpture

Activity Eight: *Circle the Correct Three Words*

1) 'Patrons' refers to individuals who support and encourage big projects such as building temples. Therefore, patrons are:

   (*Beggars, Generous rulers, Large-hearted queens, Rich merchants, Thieves*)

2) 'Builders' refers to those who actually design and construct temples and other big projects. Therefore, builders are:

   (*Masons, Sculptors, Tailors, Soldiers, Sailors, Architects*)

3) 'Dynasty of Kings' refers to a series of kings who are more or less from the same family. Therefore, a dynasty of kings is:

   (*Grandfather-father-son, Uncle-friend-pet, Student-teacher-principal*)

Temples at Khajuraho

Sometimes temples look like mountains and mountains look like temples. In fact, the high peak of a mountain is called a shikhara and the tall tower of a temple is also called a shikhara. Look at the side view of the Kandarya Mahadeva Temple: it looks like a series of Himalayan peaks—small, medium, tall.

Just as tall mountain peaks rise above the clouds and seem to touch the heavens, so also temple shikharas rise upwards and seem to touch the abode of the gods.

Actually, gods have many homes. One is deep inside our heart, the other is deep inside a temple. Our heart is protected by our body—bones, muscles, and skin. In a similar manner, the god inside the temple is protected by walls. Just as we take care of our body and beautify it, so also a temple building is well cared for and beautified. A temple is adorned by making many carvings on the walls, pillars, and beams.

Khajuraho is a small town in Madhya Pradesh and has clusters of temples that are splendid and over 1,000 years old.

Activity One: *Point to Khajuraho*

TEMPLES AT KHAJURAHO

INDIAN INDEPENDENCE DAY

Activity Two: *Compare and Match*

Human bodies and temples have similar parts and similar names.

Look at the drawing and then match Group A with Group B.

Group A

1) Thigh of a temple
2) Head of a temple
3) Foot of a temple
4) Chest of a temple
5) Neck of a temple
6) Ankle of a temple
7) Womb of a temple
8) Shoulder of a temple
9) Platform of a temple

Group B

a) is called griva.
b) is called urushringa.
c) is called garbhagriha.
d) is called khura.
e) is called jangha.
f) is called amalaka.
g) is called pada.
h) is called jagati or pitha.
i) is called skanda.

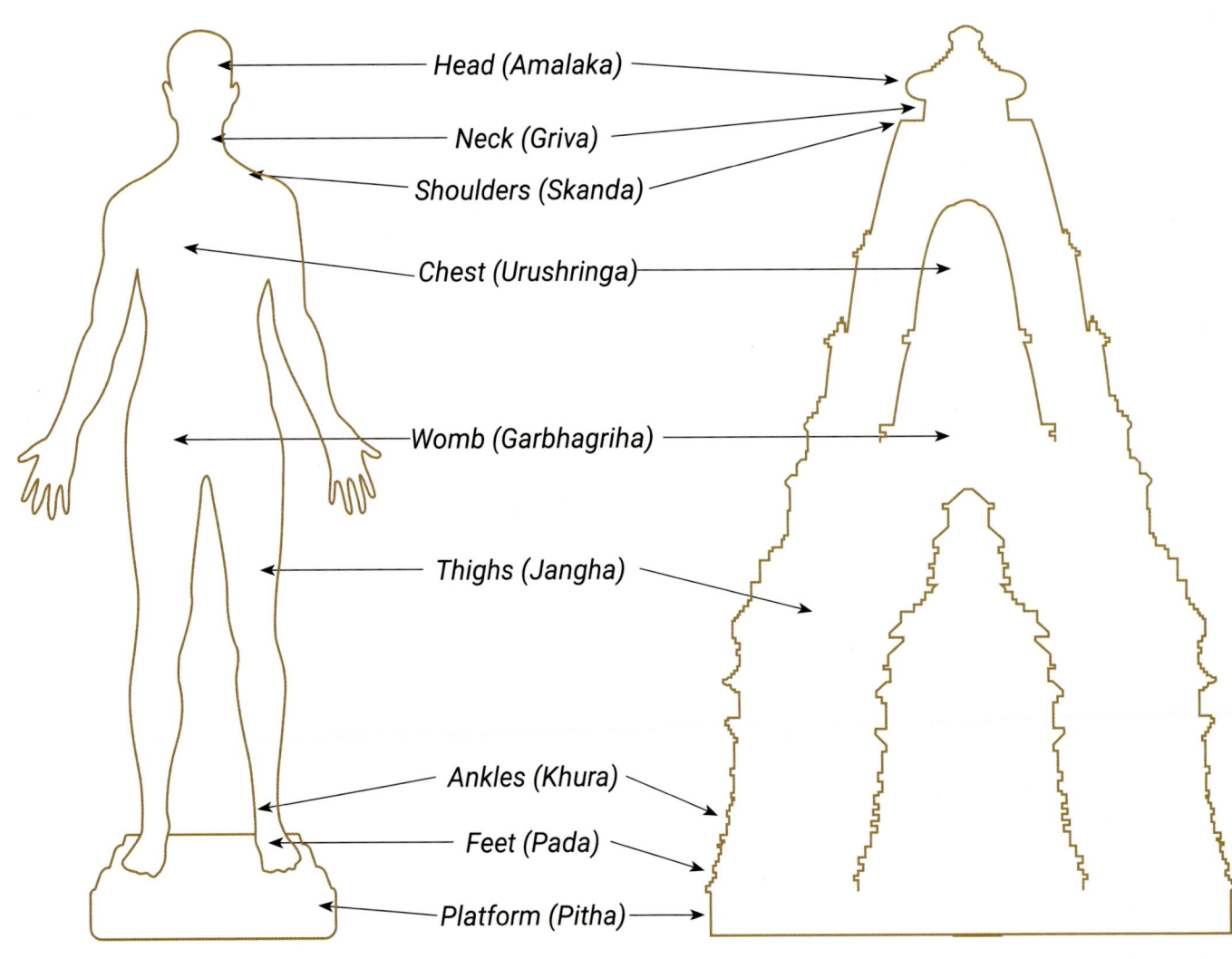

Activity Three: *Identify and Match*

1) Human footprints   2) Animal footprints   3) Temple footprint

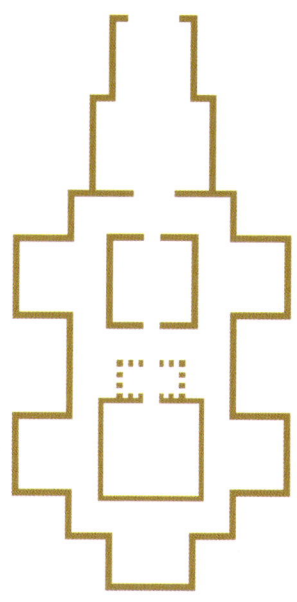
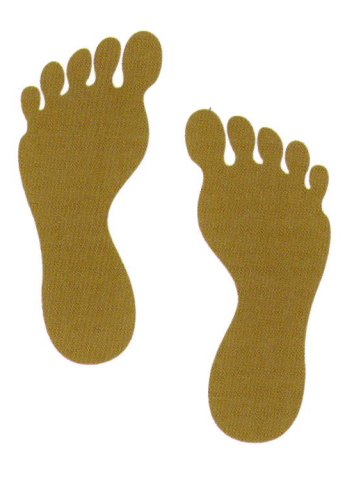

Activity Four: *Magic Square*

A magic square is etched at the entrance of the Lakshmana Temple.

In the following squares, add the numbers:

a) horizontally = _____
b) vertically = _____
c) diagonally = _____
d) at the corners = _____

7	12	1	14
2	13	8	11
16	3	10	5
9	6	15	4

7	12	1	14
2	13	8	11
16	3	10	5
9	6	15	4

7	12	1	14
2	13	8	11
16	3	10	5
9	6	15	4

7	12	1	14
2	13	8	11
16	3	10	5
9	6	15	4

Activity Five: *Vyala and Makara—Identify and Label*

Vyala and makara are strange creatures; in fact, they are a mix of many animals. Sculptures of vyala and makara are usually large, and are found in many temples at Khajuraho.

Identify the different animals that are mixed into one creature!

There are at least three animals mixed in each. Choose from the list below:

Lion	Tiger	Wolf	Dog	Rhinoceros	Horse
Elephant	Parrot	Snake	Monkey	Boar	Eagle
Ram	Deer	Crocodile	Fish	Worm	
Bull					

Activity Six: *Recognize*

Hundreds of scenes from well-known stories are sculpted on the walls of the temples. A few scenes are drawn below.

Number each scene.

1) Mother and child.

2) A heavenly maiden, called apsara, removing a thorn from her foot.

3) Dwarf, known as gana.

4) A romantic couple.

5) Woman writing a letter.

Rani-Ki-Vav at Patan

Stepwells are unique structures where one can walk all the way down to the water using steps and pathways. The grandest stepwell is the Rani-ki-vav located in Patan, Gujarat. It is seven storeys deep and very wide, and while descending one goes past hundreds of lovely carvings of animals, birds, trees, human figures, gods, goddesses, and geometrical patterns.

The carvings appear on the inner walls of the stepwell, and on beams and pillars along the walkways. Sandstone is the material used for all the construction and carvings.

This stepwell was built about 1,000 years ago but thereafter the ornamented shaft filled up with mud—perhaps due to floods—and everybody forgot about this exquisite site.

However, a few pillars and a deep water shaft could be seen. Thus, in 1940, the government ordered that the area be dug up and explored. Gradually, all the mud was removed and a wonder emerged! It is believed that Queen Udayamati had Rani-ki-vav built in memory of her husband.

| 600 | 700 | 800 | 900 | 1000 | 1083 | 1100 | 1200 | 1300 | 1400 | 1500 | 1600 | 1700 | 1800 | 1900 | 2000 |

RANI KI VAV

INDIAN INDEPENDENCE DAY

Activity One: *Point to Patan*

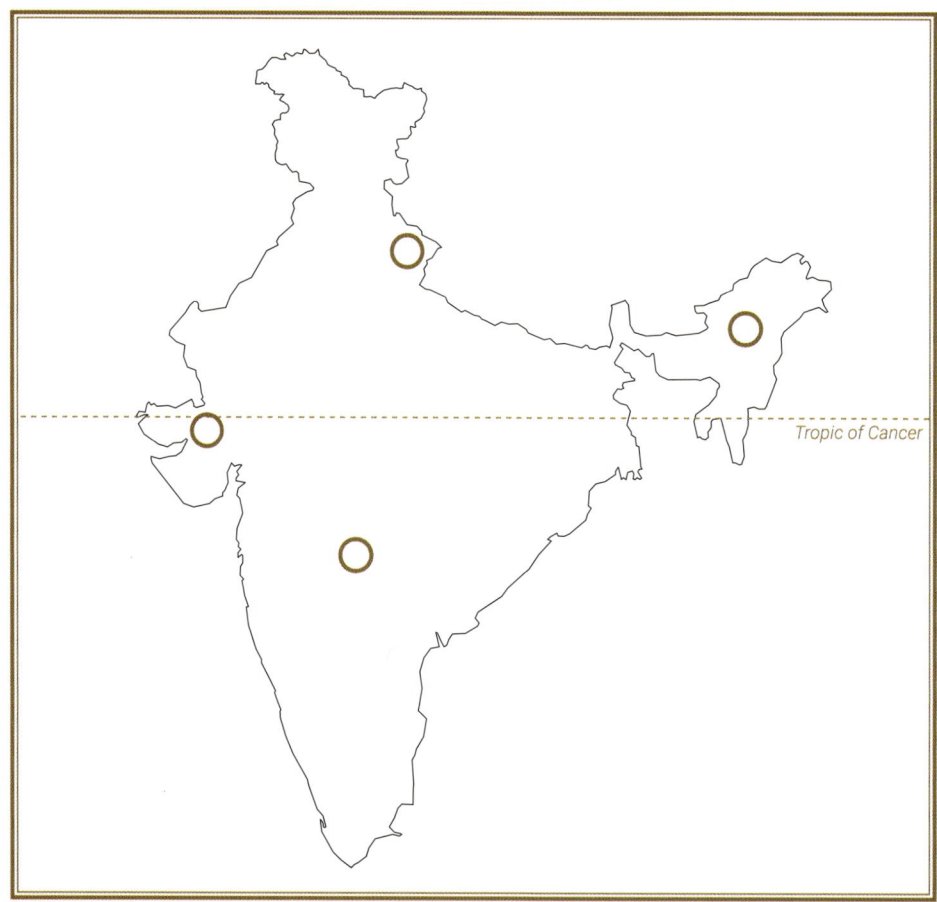

Activity Two: *Match the Following*

Group A	Group B
1) Stepwells are also called	a) is like an inverted (upside down) temple.
2) The shape of the Rani-ki-vav	b) vav or bavadi.
3) Pink is the colour	c) is a soft material.
4) Sandstone	d) of the sandstone at Rani-ki-vav.
5) About one thousand sculptures	e) are carved in the Rani-ki-vav.

Activity Three: *True or False*

1) Rani-ki-vav is shown on hundred-rupee notes in India. [T / F]

2) When the Rani-ki-vav was rediscovered in modern times, the sculptures were in very good condition because they had been buried and undisturbed for a long time. [T / F]

Activity Four: *Multiple Choice*

1) Inside the deep core of the temple, there is an image of a god. Inside the deep core of the Rani-ki-vav, there is:
(*water, towel, soap*)

2) The above fact shows that water is very valuable and needs to be:
(*protected, wasted, made dirty*)

Activity Five: *Kirtimukhas*

These motifs are known as _____ (*kirtimukhas, mangoes*) where 'kirti' means glory and 'mukha' means _____ (*face, kitchen*). Kirtimukhas are usually seen at _____ (*playground, temple*) entrances serving as _____ (*doorbells, guardians*). These faces have _____ (*bulging, tiny*) eyes, _____ (*horns, toenails*), and _____ (*legs, fangs*) and are _____ (*lion-like, turtle-like*) to behold.

Activity Six: *Fill in the Blanks*

This sculpture is found at the very bottom of the well, barely above the water.

What do you see?

1) It shows the god _____ (*Vishnu, Ganesha*) lying on the body of a many-headed _____ (*snake, boy*) called Ananta, who is floating on _____ (*water, sand*).

This sculpture of a maiden is found on the wall of the well.

What do you see?

2) This lady is arranging her hair and _____ (*looking at herself in a mirror, holding a chapati*).

70

Activity Seven: *Identify*

Image 1:

a) Goddess Durga, twenty-armed
b) Buffalo
c) Lion
d) Durga's trident

Image 2 (Right):

a) Lotus pedestals
b) Rishi with his arms raised
c) The god Vishnu
d) Chakra on Vishnu's finger
e) Conch shell
f) Surasundari playing the flute
g) Kirtimukhas

Image 3 (Left):

a) Mango leaves
b) Surasundari reaching for mangoes
c) Parrot
d) Jewellery

Great Living Chola Temples
at Tamil Nadu

The kings of the Chola kingdom were powerful. They ruled all of South India and even the neighbouring islands. They ruled for a very long time—one great Chola king followed another—and they are remembered for the many good things that they did.

About 900 to 1,000 years ago, they built three grand temples in Tamil Nadu: the Brihadeshvara Temple at Thanjavur, the Brihadeshvara Temple at Gangaikondacholapuram, and the Airavatesvara Temple at Darasuram. All the temples were built in the Dravida mode using very hard granite stone.

These are called the Great Living Chola Temples because they are grand and majestic with many sculptures, paintings, and bronze statues, and they are just as lively today as they were long ago. Many worshippers come and go. Men, women, and children

Activity One: *Point to Thanjavur*

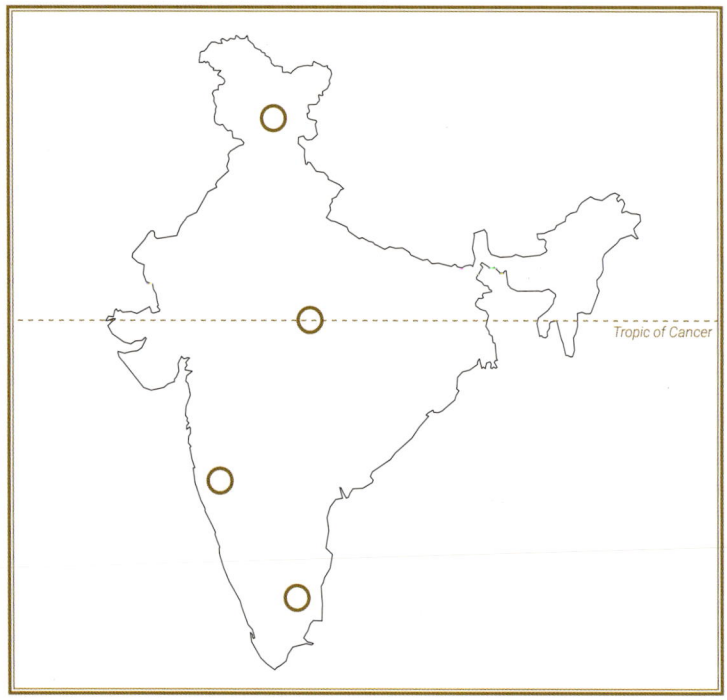

neatly dressed arrive with flowers and gifts for the gods, and old customs are still followed.

The sound of musical instruments and the recitation of sacred chants fill the air. Energetic performances and processions are held to please the deities and visitors. Priests, pilgrims, and others criss-cross the large grounds and rest in the covered areas.

GREAT LIVING CHOLA TEMPLES

INDIAN INDEPENDENCE DAY

The Brihadeshvara Temple at Thanjavur is the tallest amongst all the temples in India. The tall temple tower, called vimana in South India, is directly above the sanctum, as always. The sanctum, more commonly known as garbhagriha, is the most holy spot. Inside the garbhagriha at the Brihadeshvara temple there is a Shiva linga. Shiva's mount, a bull called Nandi, is seated patiently outside the temple entrance; this Nandi is carved from stone.

Like most Dravida mode South Indian temples, the Brihadeshvara Temple is enclosed within a vast courtyard. A lengthy, semi-covered corridor wraps around the courtyard. This corridor is called prakara and it has many beautifully engraved pillars. This passageway where visitors can rest also has several sub-shrines dedicated to different gods. At the Brihadeshvara Temple, there are sub-shrines dedicated to the eight dikpalas, guardians of the eight directions.

In addition to this, it is a pleasure to discover eighty-one Bharatnatyam dance poses carved on the walls of the main temple. Visitors enter this temple complex through an impressive gateway called a gopuram.

Activity Two: *Match the Following*

Group A | Group B

1) A gopuram is a gateway shaped

2) The height of the Brihadeshvara

3) Asta dikpala

4) Sculptures can be made of

a) stone, bronze, wood, and other materials.

b) like the head of a cow with horns.

c) Temple at Thanjavur is probably 59.82 metres.

d) means 'guardians of the eight directions'.

Activity Three: *Name the Directions*

1) South

2) West

3) North-west

4) South-east

5) North-east

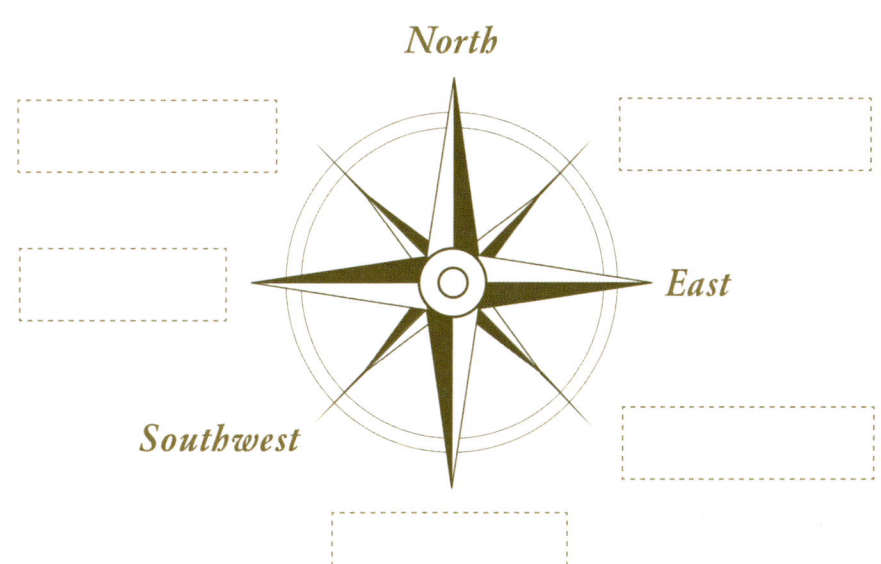

Activity Four: *Identify the Correct Shape of a Shiva Linga*

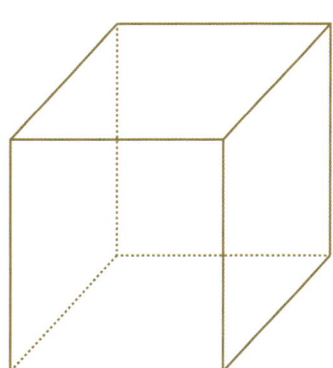
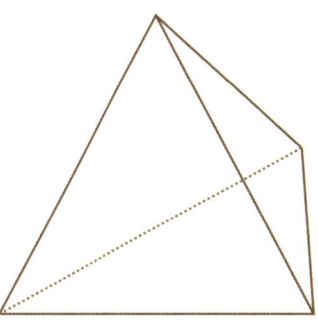

Brihadeshvara Temple at Gangaikondacholapuram

Once, the Chola King Rajendra I went northwards and conquered the areas near the Ganga River. He then returned to South India and called himself the great Gangai-konda-cholan, meaning 'the one who conquered the Ganga'. Next, he developed a city called Gangaikondacholapuram. Here, he built a grand temple called the Brihadeshvara Temple. It was very similar to the one his father, King Rajaraja I, had built nearby in Thanjavur. It even had the same name. While this new temple also had a large courtyard, a long prakara, a tall vimana, a big Shiva linga in the garbhagriha, and a massive Nandi outside, it was altogether on a smaller scale than the Brihadeshvara Temple in Thanjavur.

Further, as at Thanjavur, the Brihadeshvara Temple at Gangaikondacholapuram, was also a centre of social, economic, and political activities in addition to being a place of worship. Cultural activities such as music, dance, and art thrived here. The temple also supported crafts such as garland making, basket weaving, jewellery making, pottery, metalwork, woodcarving and more.

Activity Five: *Match the Following*

Group A

1) Calculating profit-loss

2) Choosing leaders, war or peace, making rules

3) Managing different types of people

Group B

a) are political activities.

b) is an economic activity.

c) is a social activity.

Activity Six: *Name the Rivers*

The Chola kings ruled around the _____

1) Kaveri River   2) Ganga River

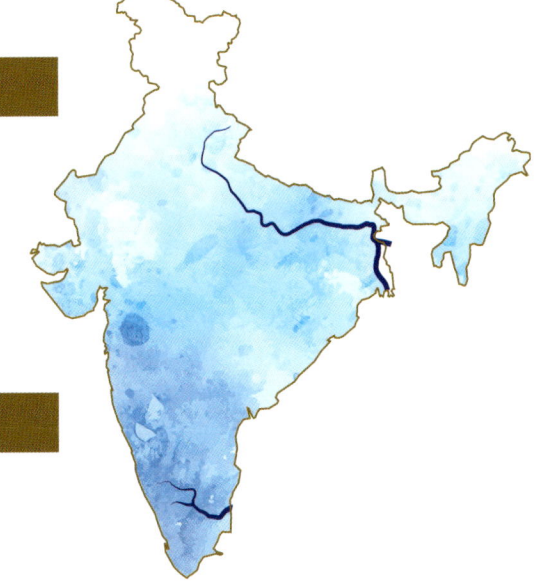

Activity Seven: *Tick the Correct Answers*

1) Five activities that happen inside a temple are:

Chanting, Rock climbing, Singing, Praying, Sweeping, Car racing, Hunting, Studying

2) Five musical instruments used in South Indian temples are:

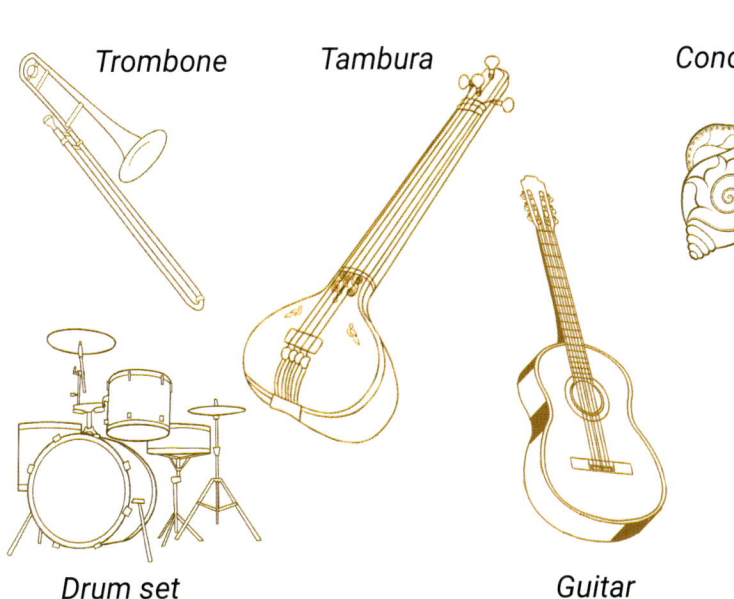

Trombone   *Tambura*

Drum set   *Guitar*

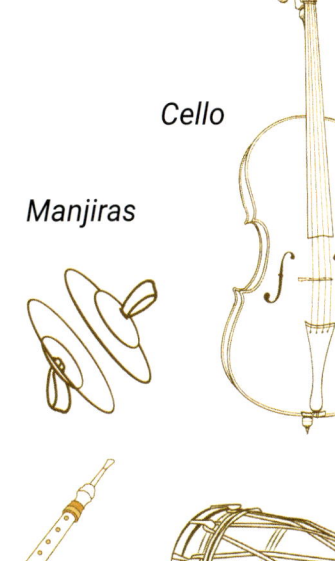

Conch   *Manjiras*   *Cello*

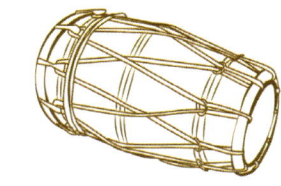

Nadaswaram   *Mridangam*

Rudreshwara Temple at Palampet

Buildings today usually have simple, rectangular floor plans upon which four-sided, box-like structures are raised. In contrast, temples in the olden days had floor plans with complex patterns and the temple structures built upon these would be multisided. Artisans and sculptors would enthusiastically decorate and carve almost every inch of these surfaces.

The Rudreshwara Temple is one such structure. Built in stone by the Kakatiya rulers in the 13th century, this temple has a star-shaped plan that gave rise to many walls. These are filled with motifs from nature and with figures engaged in dance. The frequent use of black dolerite stone that is polished to shine like metal is a unique feature of this temple. Brackets with life-size dancing figures sculpted in dolerite adorn the porch of the temple.

A tall vimana was built in the Vesara mode of architecture using lightweight, porous bricks; the Kakatiyas were the only kingdom in this era to use these innovative bricks. A long inscription detailing the glory of the Kakatiya kings is also present at the temple.

While many skilled craftspersons and engineers worked at building this temple, the chief sculptor was called Ramappa and therefore this temple, near Warangal in Telangana, is also known as the Ramappa Temple. Last but not least, this temple is set in a wide open space amongst fields, a forest, and a lake.

Activity One: *Point to Palampet*

Qutub Minar Complex at Delhi

The Qutub Minar is the tallest and the most magnificent tower in India. It was built as a tower of victory to mark the establishment of a new Islamic polity in India in 1192 CE. In subsequent years, new Islamic kingdoms and empires were founded across South Asia.

The Qutub Minar is in Delhi and is located inside a compound that has many Islamic style monuments, all from different time periods. Today, this collection is called the Qutub Complex.

The Qutub Minar is probably named after a saint called Qutubuddin Kaki. This tower has five distinct storeys. It is red because a lot of red sandstone has been used for building; some white marble has been used for the top storeys. Inside, there are 397 steps. The minar has decorative motifs carved on the walls that are considered Islamic in flavour such as geometrical patterns, floral patterns, and stylishly-written verses from the Quran and other texts.

Soon after the Qutub Minar was built, a stately doorway to enter the Qutub Complex was added by Sultan Allauddin of the Khilji dynasty. This doorway is called the Alai Darwaza. Here, additional Islamic features were added such as a dome and arches. Allauddin also began the construction of a minar that was to be twice the size of the Qutub Minar, but he died before it could be completed. This unfinished minar is called the Alai Minar.

Activity One: Point to Delhi

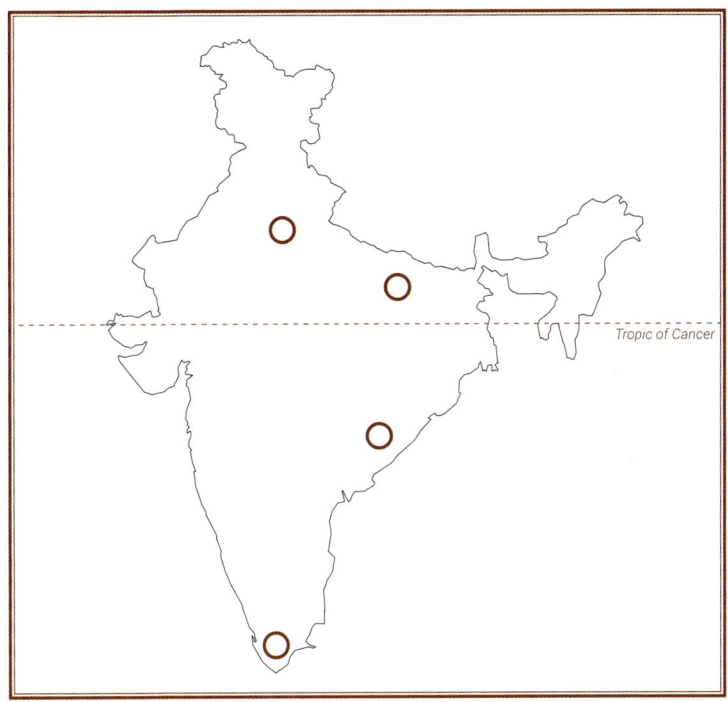

Activity Two: Find the Words

1) Minar
2) Darwaza
3) Islamic
4) Khilji
5) Sultan
6) Ghori
7) Quran

Y	Y	Y	X	X	X	X	X	X
Y	Y	Y	M	I	N	A	R	X
K	H	I	L	J	I	V	V	X
Y	D	A	R	W	A	Z	A	X
Y	X	X	X	V	V	V	V	X
Y	X	X	X	G	H	O	R	I
I	S	L	A	M	I	C	Z	Z
Y	V	V	V	Q	U	R	A	N
V	V	S	U	L	T	A	N	Z

600 700 800 900 1000 1100 **1192** 1200 1300 **1320** 1400 1500 1600 1700 1800 1900 2000

QUTUB MINAR COMPLEX   INDIAN INDEPENDENCE DAY

Activity Three: *Locate on the Site Map*

Look at the site map and label the monuments.

1) Qutub Minar 2) Alai Minar 3) Iron Pillar 4) Alai Darwaza 5) Quwwat-ul-Islam Masjid 6) Tomb of Iman Zamin

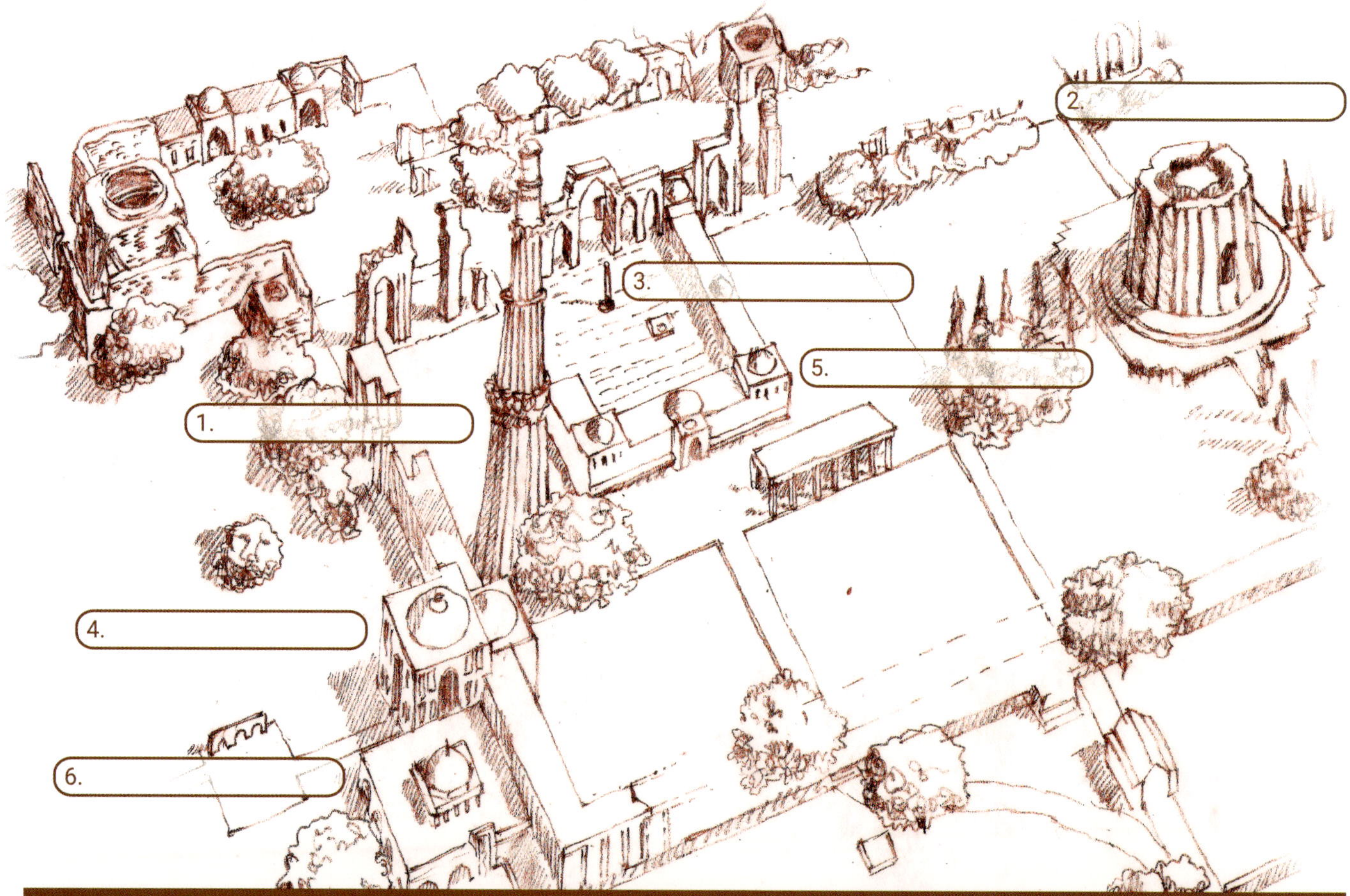

Activity Four: *Point out Screens Using Arrows (at least six)*

Tomb of Iman Zamin: Iman Zamin was an important Islamic religious leader. Before he died, he had an elegant little house built and wished to be buried inside it. It was airy with many screens called jalis.

Exterior *Interior*

Activity Five: *Recognize and Label the Motifs*

On the surface of the Qutub Minar, there are all kinds of patterns, motifs, and designs.

1) Hexagonal geometric patterns.

2) Stylishly-written verses from the Koran.

3) Floral patterns such as:
(a) Large yellow lotus
(b) Creepers with round flowers
(c) Leaves
(d) Combination of all these

Activity Six: *Multiple Choice—Iron Pillar*

A pillar is raised to signify victory. At the Qutub Complex, proud Islamic rulers displayed a tall Iron Pillar in addition to the lofty sandstone minar. This Iron Pillar is actually much older than the Qutub Minar, and was probably taken from Madhya Pradesh and brought to Delhi. This pillar causes much wonder because it has not rusted although 1,600 years have passed since it was forged. An ancient inscription on the pillar in the Gupta script informs us that it was made to remember King Chandra and Lord Vishnu.

1) The Iron Pillar has been inspired by:

    a) a lotus flower and stalk
    b) a mountain
    c) a bow and arrow

2) The ancient Gupta script looks like this:

3) The Iron Pillar is about 23 feet high. The Qutub Minar is about 237 feet high. How many 'Iron Pillars' need to be joined to make a tower as high as the Qutub Minar?

    a) about 5
    b) about 10
    c) about 20

Activity Seven: *Point Out—Quwwat-ul-Islam*

Located near the Qutub Minar is the mosque called Quwwat-ul-Islam, which means the Might of Islam. Within the mosque's compound, there is an Iron Pillar and also the tombs of several powerful Islamic rulers. There is a hall made by reusing pillars from Hindu and Jain temples. Notably, these pillars display indic motifs such as temple bells, mango leaves, and human figures.

1) Pillars from Hindu and Jain temples

2) Dome

3) Hall where people can gather and pray

4) Minar

Archaeological Park at Champaner-Pavagadh

Located in Gujarat, Champaner is a town in the plains and Pavagadh is on a hill that towers above. Five million years ago, this hill was a volcano spewing fire and smoke. Many prehistoric and historic remains are scattered throughout this landscape. This is why it is called an archaeological park.

While people have lived in this area since very ancient times, it became popular between the eighth century and sixteenth century CE when rulers such as Vanraj Chavda and Mahmud Begada settled here and built many grand structures.

Forts were built, rebuilt, and expanded; their walls stretched from the hills to the plains. Jain and Hindu temples were built on the hill; mosques, tombs and palaces were built in the plains; and well-designed water structures were built everywhere.

Champaner is famous particularly for being an old, planned city, for the delicate carvings on monuments, and for a unique architectural style that blends Hindu, Muslim, and Jain designs. Reddish-yellow limestone, which is fairly easy to cut, was the building material available here. However, in 1535 CE, the Mughal emperor Humayun sacked this sprawling city; the residents fled never to return. Regardless, pilgrimages to the Hindu and Jain shrines at Pavagadh have continued for hundreds of years.

ARCHAEOLOGICAL PARK AT CHAMPANER-PAVAGADH

INDIAN INDEPENDENCE DAY

Activity One: *Join the Dots—Discover Champaner*

Build the city of Champaner.

Sakar Khan's Tomb

Portion of the city wall

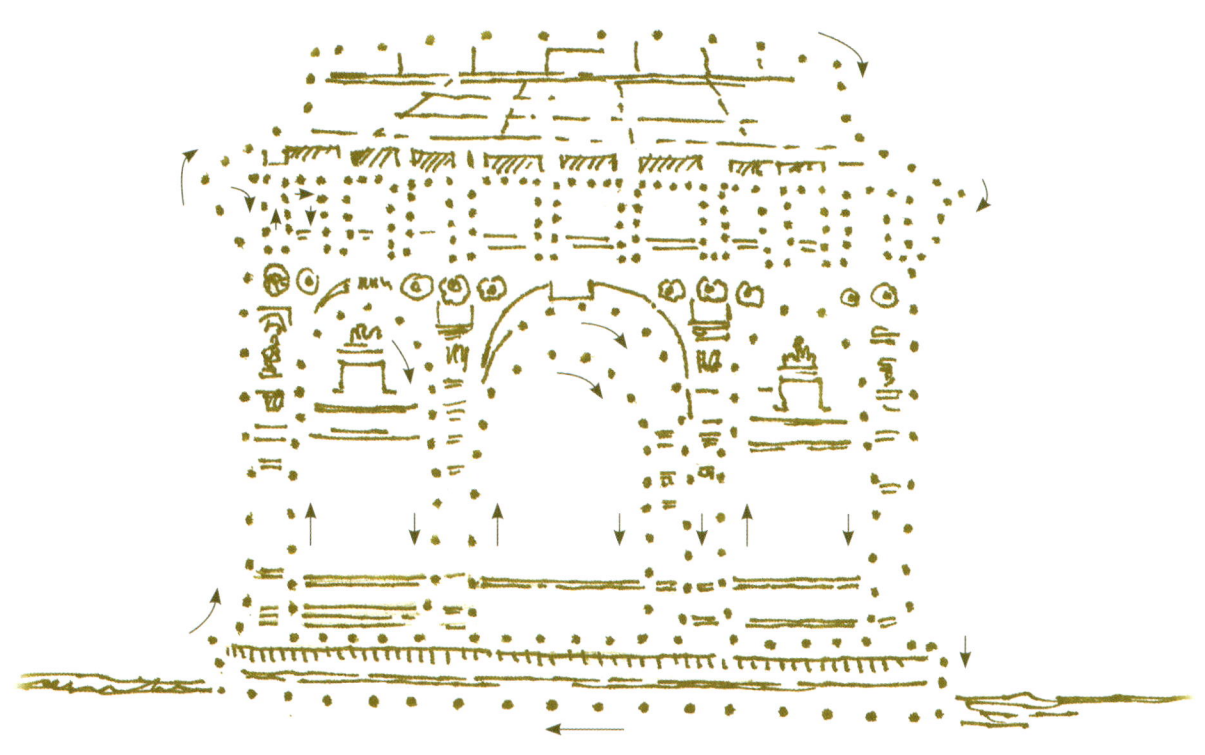

Tomb in the Nagina Masjid Complex

Jami Masjid

Activity Two: Point to Champaner-Pavagadh

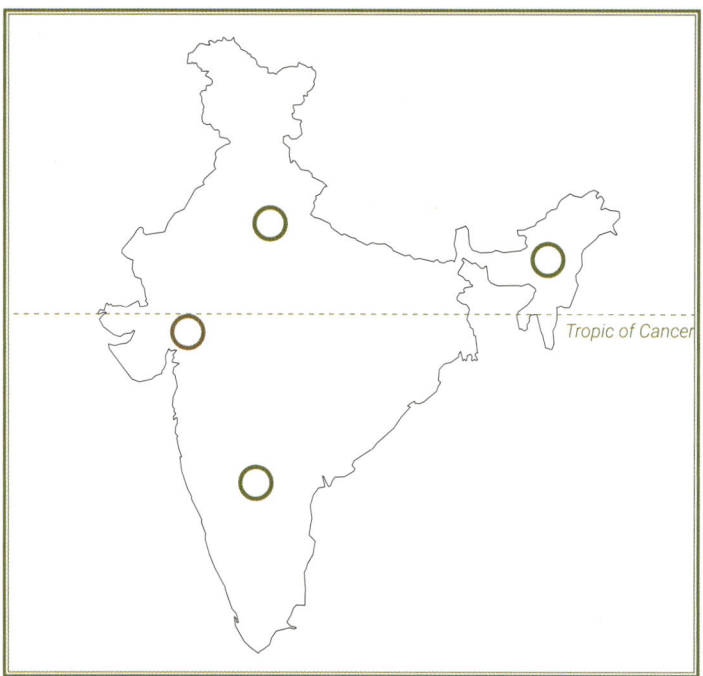

Activity Three: Multiple Choice

1) Champaner was an important city of the
(*Gujarat Sultanate, Delhi Sultanate, Bengal Sultanate*).

2) Scribbling on the surfaces of monuments or leaving behind
(*graffiti, confetti, serengeti*) is a very (*uncaring, good, right*) thing to do.

Activity Four: Match the Following

Group A

1) Archaeologists unearth

2) Geologists study

3) Environmentalists

4) Art historians understand

5) The Archaeological Survey of India,

Group B

a) earth and all its layers.

b) conserve nature.

c) objects that belong to the past.

d) ASI, cares for monuments.

e) history by studying art and architecture, as you are doing in this workbook.

Activity Five: *Colour the Timeline on Pages 87 and 88 of Champaner-Pavagadh*

1) Colour 400 BCE and older as blue.

2) Colour eighth century CE to sixteenth century CE as green (that is, 701 CE to 1599 CE).

3) Colour second century BCE to sixth century CE as yellow (that is, 199 BCE to 599 CE).

Activity Six : *Colour the Water Cycle*

Rain that fell on the Pavagadh hills was carefully held in ponds and lakes. Eventually, it seeped downwards or was intentionally channelled downwards to the plains of Champaner where it would appear in the wells and tanks. Due to good management, these towns had enough water in the past. In more recent times, the wisdom of old water structures and systems has not been understood, and they have been neglected.

Colour all water as blue, colour the vegetation as green.

Sun Temple at Konark

Buildings are of many shapes and sizes. Imagine a large stone building shaped like a chariot with wheels and stone horses attached to the front. This is the astonishing form of the Konark Temple in Odisha dedicated to the sun god, Surya. It is believed that Surya rides across the sky in a chariot, and this temple is built to look like Surya's chariot.

The Konark Temple was built in the thirteenth century. Over time its shikhara became weak and toppled. The main idol of Surya disappeared as well—it was perhaps destroyed or looted by invaders. Thereafter, worshippers stopped coming to this temple and it became increasingly neglected.

Now however, people are returning to this monument. They are studying the few surviving portions such as the dance hall and the assembly hall, and also appreciating the skill of the artisans and the scientific knowledge of the builders. Visitors are discovering many secrets about this place such as the fact that the wheels of the chariot are actually ancient clocks called sundials. Moreover, Surya's chariot has twelve pairs of wheels to remind us that there are twelve months in a year; there are seven horses attached to the sun god's chariot to recall the seven days of the week and also the seven colours of the rainbow.

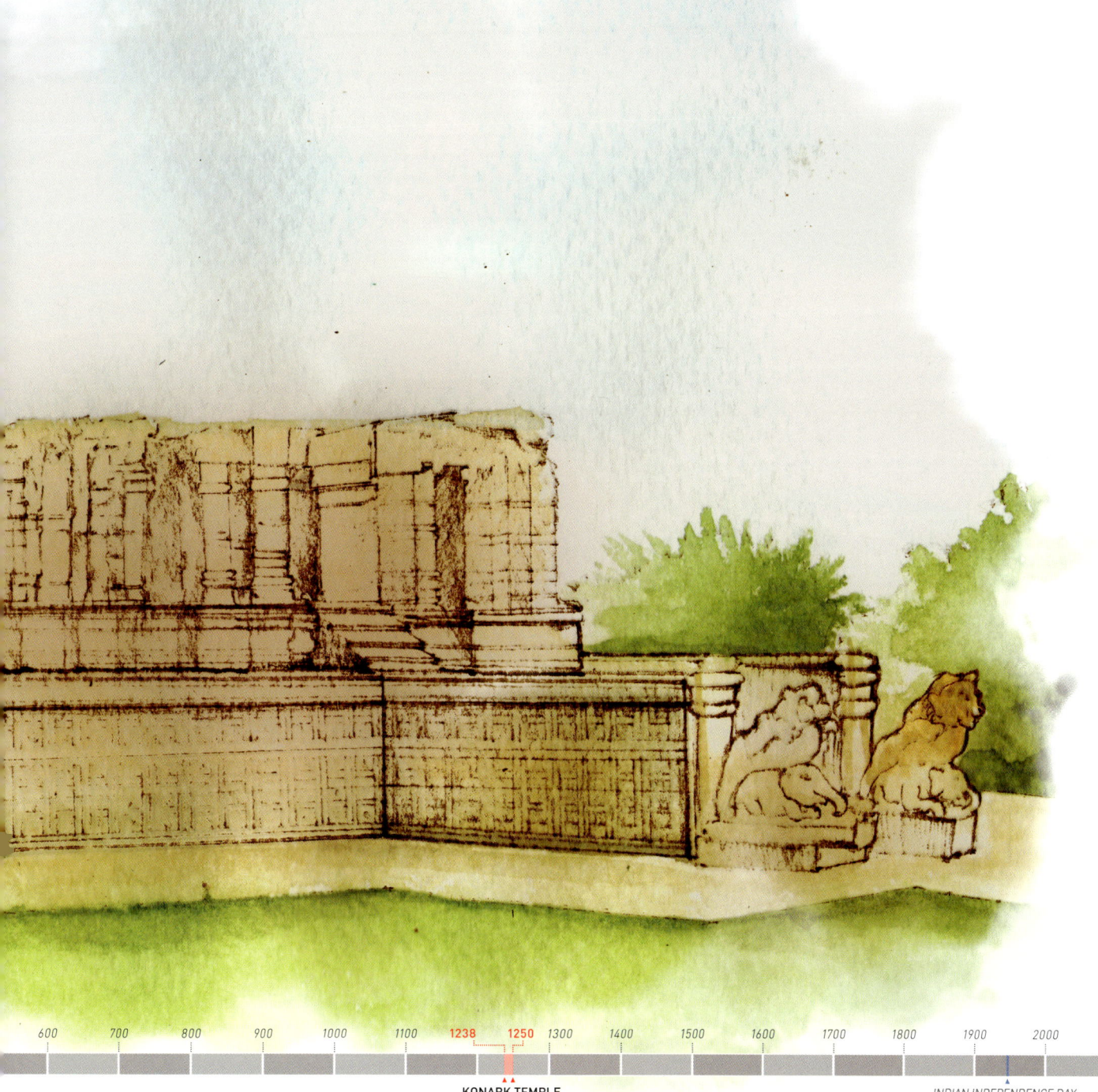

Activity One: *Point to Konark*

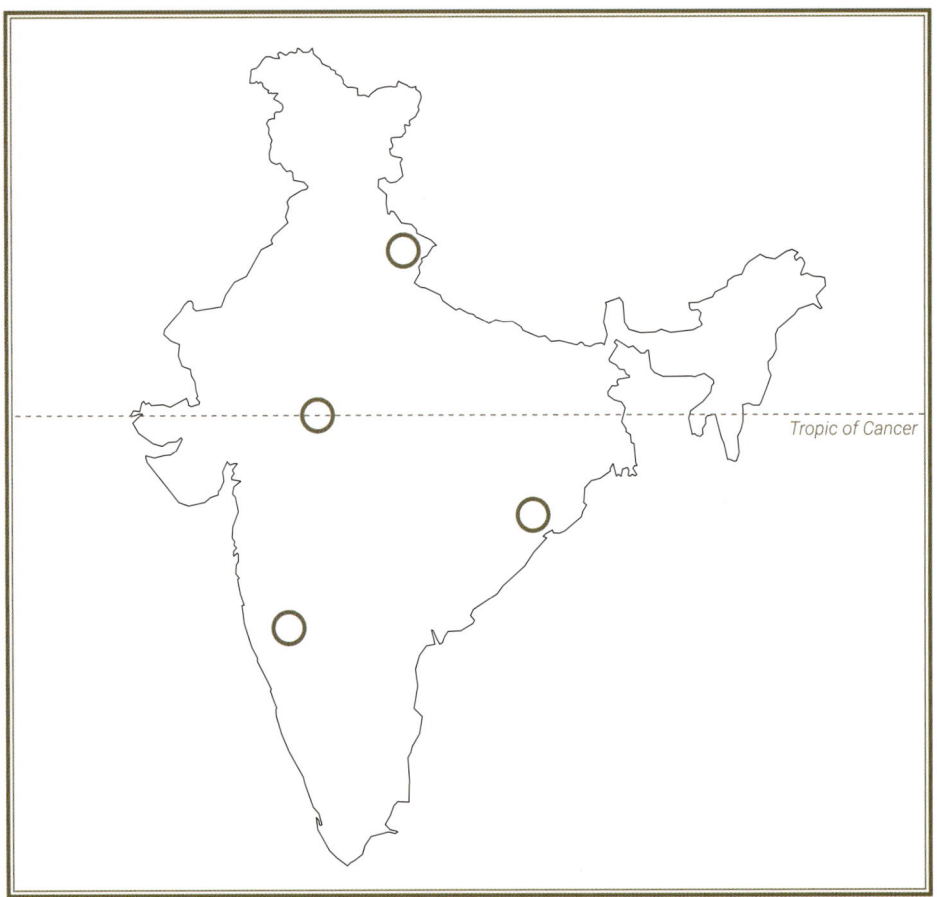

Activity Two: *Multiple Choice*

1) The dotted portion of the temple has fallen down, therefore what remains?
   a) Shikhara
   b) Jagmohan
   c) Gopuram

2) The jagmohan is probably:
   a) a space where worshippers gather
   b) a place for horses to live
   c) a place to store old jugs

3) What is a shikhara?
   a) Platform
   b) Tower
   c) Gate

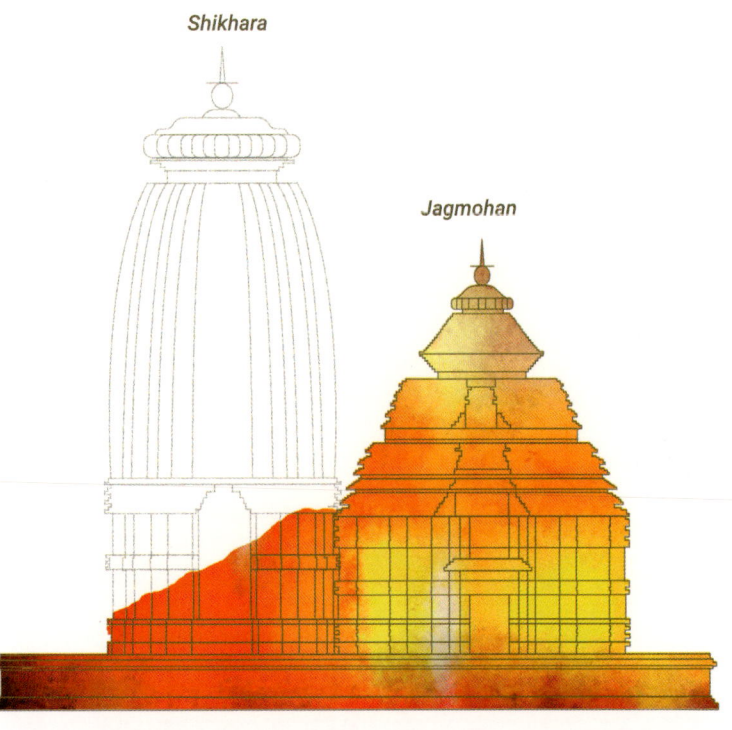

Activity Three: Match the Following

Group A

1) The temple walls have carvings of

2) The twenty-four wheels of the temple

3) Khondalite, chlorite, and laterite

4) The Great Wheel at Konark appears

Group B

a) are also sundials by which one can tell time.

b) are types of stone used to build the temple.

c) on ten-rupee notes in India.

d) animals such as elephants, lions, and snakes.

Activity Four: Cross Out

From the list below, cross out five things NOT present in this panel.

Leaf

Bird

Baby camel

Elephant

Ship

Temple

Cow

Lamp

Giraffe

Flower

People

Activity Five: *Colour the Temple*

1) Khondalite stone (pinkish colour) was used for constructing most of the temple.

2) Chlorite stone (greenish colour) was used for the door frames and a few sculptures.

3) Laterite stone (reddish colour) was used for the foundation and for the staircases.

Activity Six: *Telling Time on a Sundial*

This wheel is a sundial. It is like a clock, but the numbers move in an anti-clockwise direction. The knob at the centre of the wheel casts a shadow. This shadow is used to tell the time.

1) Colour the a.m. portion of the sundial.

2) Colour the p.m. portion of the sundial in a different colour.

3) How many thick spokes are there in this wheel?

4) What is the duration of time between two thick spokes?

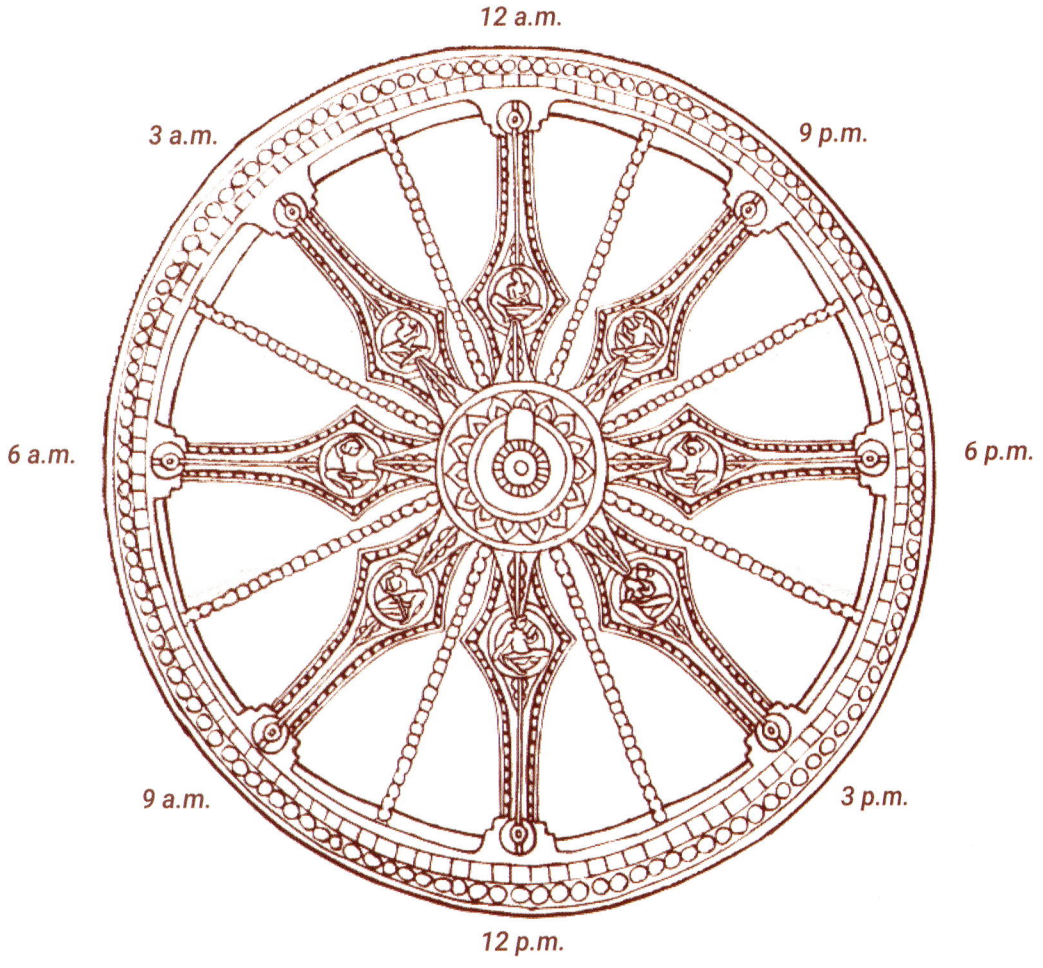

Activity Seven: *True or False*

1) The sundial uses the sun and not batteries. [T / F]

2) The sundial has the same markings as a clock. [T / F]

3) The sundial cannot be used at night or when it is cloudy. [T / F]

4) The sundial rings like an alarm clock. [T / F]

Monuments at Hampi

Hampi was a expansive, rich, and progressive city that was the centre of the Vijayanagara empire for 200 years. Then in 1565 CE, it was conquered, looted, and burnt by their competitors, the sultans of the Deccan.

Now, about 1,600 ruined structures lie silently along the Tungabhadra River, amongst rocky hills in Karnataka. These remains tell us a story of people who loved art, were religious, skilfully practised farming, and had bustling markets and clever defence systems.

Activity Two: *Point to Hampi*

Tropic of Cancer

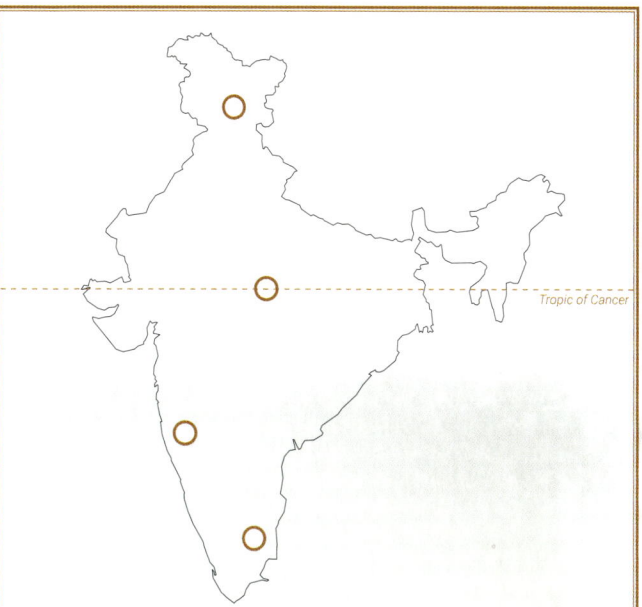

Activity One: *Identify and Label*

1) Matanga Hill

2) Virupaksha Temple Complex

3) Rocky hills

1.
2.

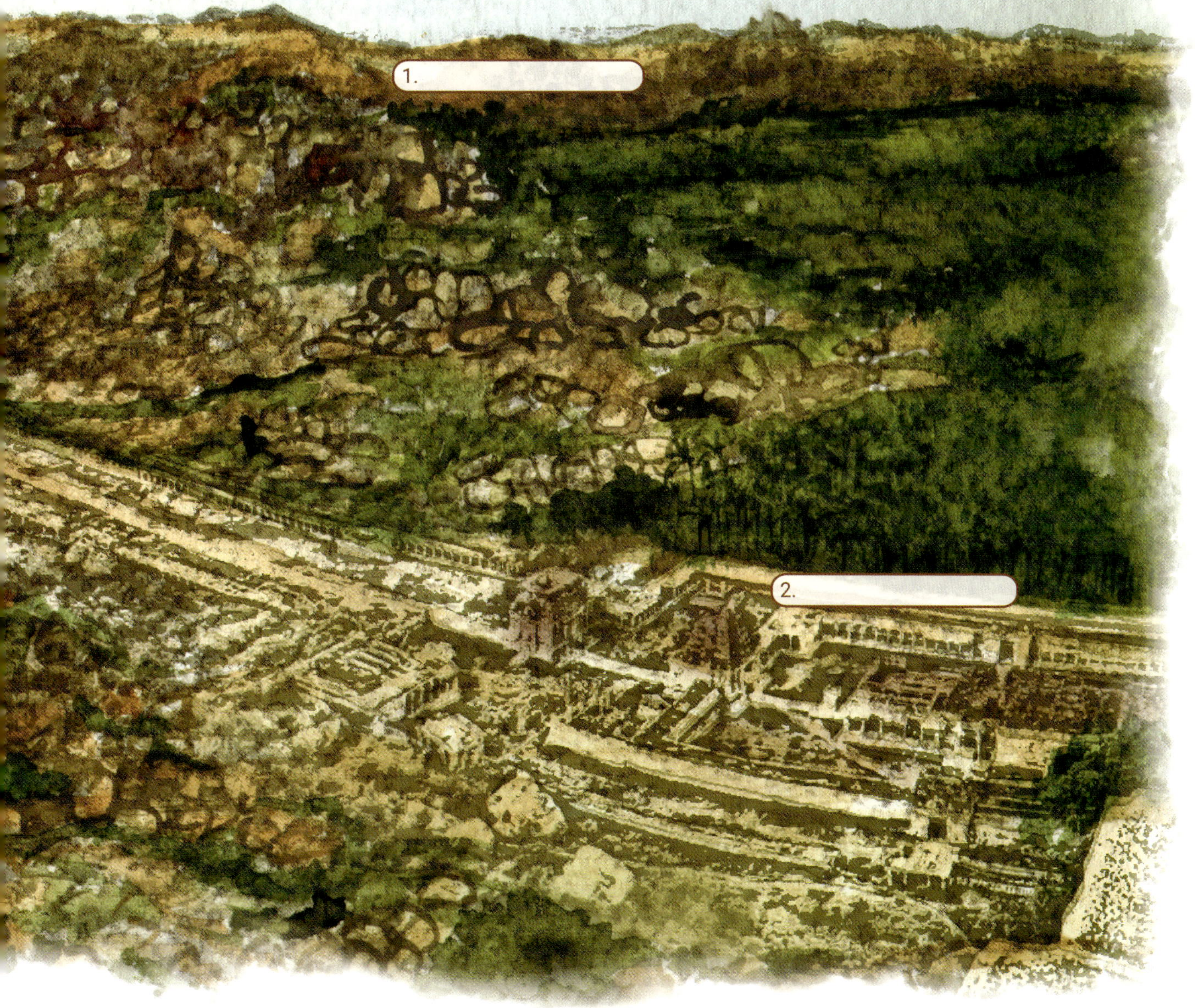

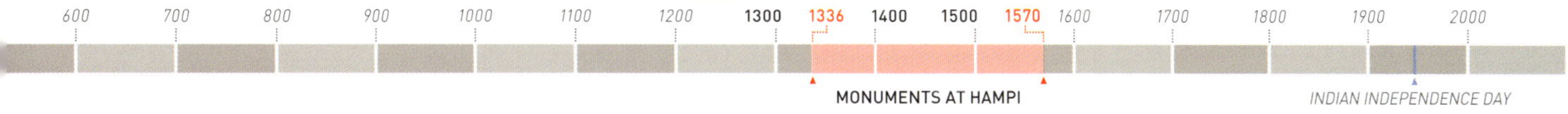

600
700
800
900
1000
1100
1200
1300
1336
1400
1500
1570
1600
1700
1800
1900
2000
MONUMENTS AT HAMPI
INDIAN INDEPENDENCE DAY

Activity Three: *Label*

1) Tungabhadra River   2) Coracle boat   3) Wooden Ratha

Activity Four: *Odd One Out*

1) Sacred structures at Hampi include:
(*Temples, Shrines, Mandapas, Gopurams, Hotels, Holy tanks*)

2) Defence systems include:
(*Pencils, Moats, Gateways, Checkposts, Watchtowers, Fort walls*)

3) Agricultural systems include:
(*Canals, Backpacks, Aqueducts, Wells, Drains, Ponds*)

4) Building materials at Hampi include:
(*Stone, Plastic, Granite, Brick, Lime, Mortar*)

5) Royal structures include:
(*Lotus Mahal, Elephant stables, Bathhouses, Cement factories, Breezy mandapas*)

Activity Five: *Tick the Right Answers*

The Virupaksha Temple is called a 'living temple' because many customs have been practised in its premises for a long time. These customs include:

1) The type of singing
2) The way of worshipping
3) The festivals and use of chariots
4) The role of the priest, cooks, garland makers
5) The constant arrival of worshippers and pilgrims
6) All of the above

Activity Six: *Multiple Choice—Ratha*

1) Ratha means (*rat, angry, chariot*).

2) At (*Hampi, Hyderabad, Himmatpur*), there is a stone shrine shaped like a ratha.

3) This stone ratha (*never moves, is very light, has an engine*).

4) At temples, wooden rathas move and are used for transporting (*gods, horses, robbers*).

5) This famous stone ratha of Hampi is shown on the (*50, 100, 2,000*) rupee note.

Activity Seven: *Match the Following*

Group A	Group B
1) King Krishnadevaraya ruled Hampi	a) produce the notes sa, re, ga, ma.
2) The Dravida mode of architecture is common	b) from 1509 CE to 1530 CE.
3) A Grand Bazaar Street (market) was often	c) in South India and at Hampi.
4) The Vijaya Vitthala Temple has	d) just outside the temple complex.
5) Stone musical pillars are tapped with fingers and	e) delicate carvings, a stone ratha, and musical pillars.

Activity Eight: *Join the Dots—Discover Hampi*

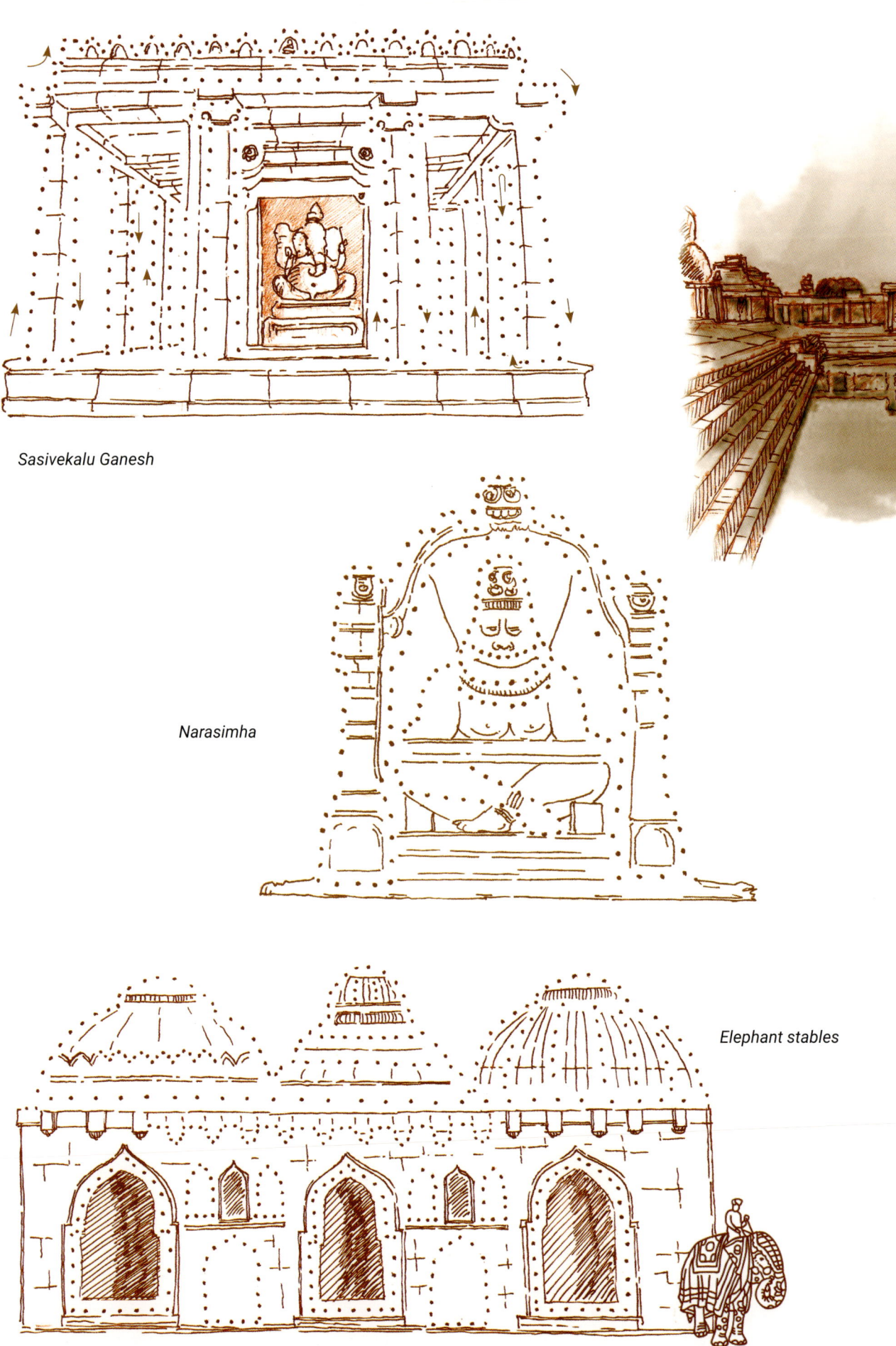

Sasivekalu Ganesh

Narasimha

Elephant stables

Hazara Ram Temple

Pushkarani temple tank

Lotus Mahal

Activity Nine: *Fill in the Blanks*

In many temples, the worshipper passes through mandapas before reaching the _____ (*sanctum, stable*). A mandapa is a covered _____ (*hole, hall*). A large hall where many might meet to watch musicians or dancers is called a _____ (*maha-mandapa, maha-rastra*); and a small space where only few people can gather, such as immediately in front of the sanctum, is called an _____ (*ardha-mandapa, ardha-navasana*). The walls and ceilings of the mandapas are well-decorated with _____ (*wings, carvings*). There are also mandapas that are full of decorated _____ (*pillars, peppers*). Or, there are solitary mandapas that are open on all sides and located at a breezy and _____ (*ugly, scenic*) spot.

Historic City of Ahmedabad

Ahmedabad is named after Sultan Ahmed Shah who established the city in approximately 1411 CE. He built a fort, now called Bhadra Fort, of which many attractively carved stone sections have survived. The fort had eight gates and inside, there were palaces, mosques, and many homes. Gradually, it became crowded and Ahmed Shah's grandson, Mahmud Begada, added an outer wall and thereby the fortified city expanded.

Later, pols developed. Here, pol means a cluster of closely packed houses with a common gateway. Many pols exist even today. Within the pol, there are narrow lanes flanked by private homes, several of which are quaint. A courtyard is a favourite feature and it could contain a bird feeder or a stepwell called vav. In a pol, there are also places of worship such as a Hindu temple, a Jain temple, or a mosque.

Ahmedabad has an astonishing number of historic structures that deserve protection and preservation. The best care is given to those on the list of the Archaeological Survey of India (ASI)—about twenty-eight of them. Besides these, there are numerous other sites that are worthy of being called 'heritage sites', but receive no special protection.

Mahatma Gandhi's residence on the banks of the Sabarmati River in Ahmedabad is well-tended and loved.

Activity One: *Label the Houses*

1) Pol House (traditional house)

2) Prayer House (mosque)

3) Deceased Person's House (tomb)

4) Bird House

5) God's House (temple)

6) House for Many People (fort)

7) Water House (vav)

8) Ruler's House (palace)

9) Mahatma Gandhi's House (Sabarmati Ashram)

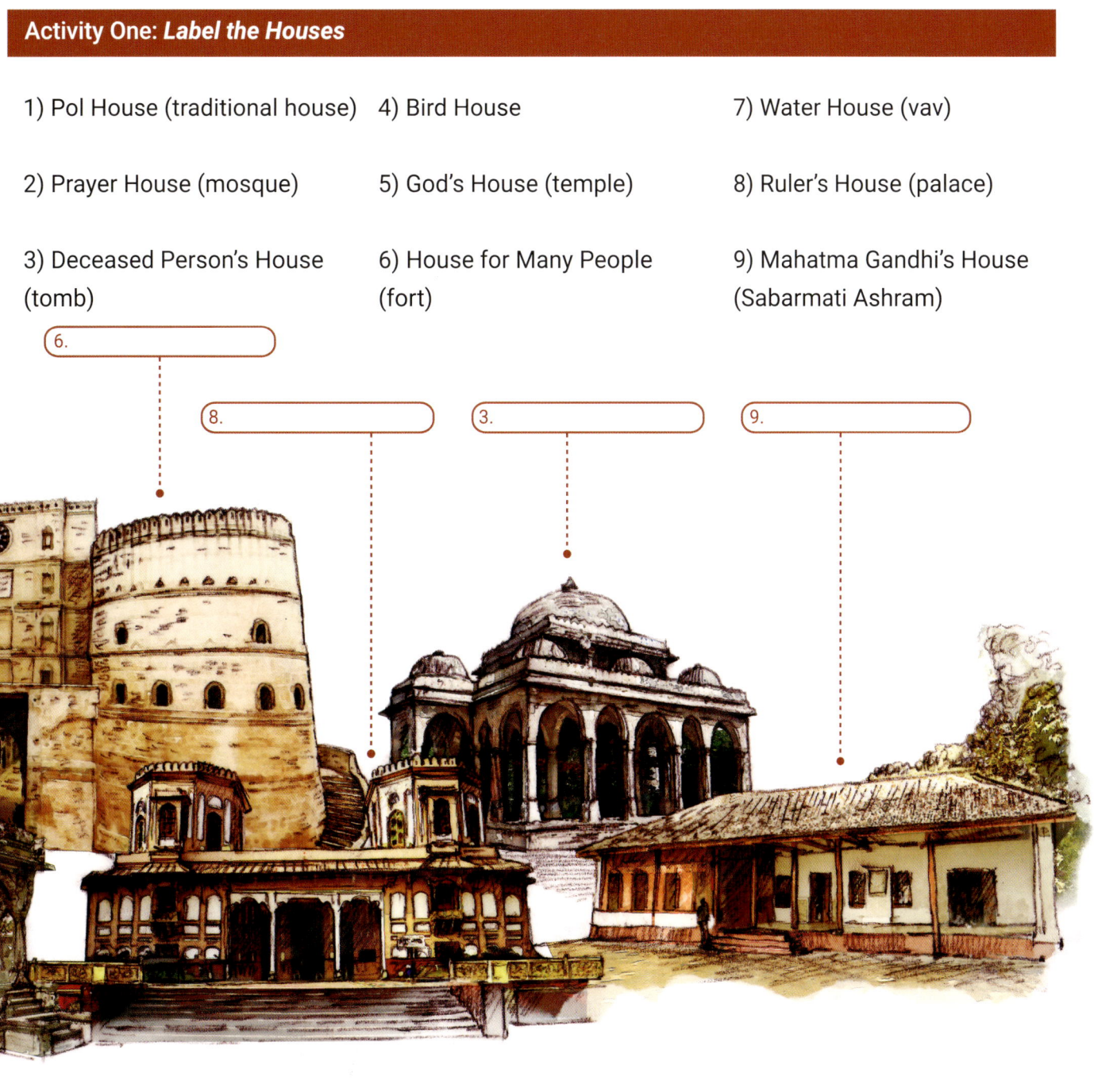

HISTORIC CITY OF AHMEDABAD

INDIAN INDEPENDENCE DAY

Activity Two: *Point to Ahmedabad*

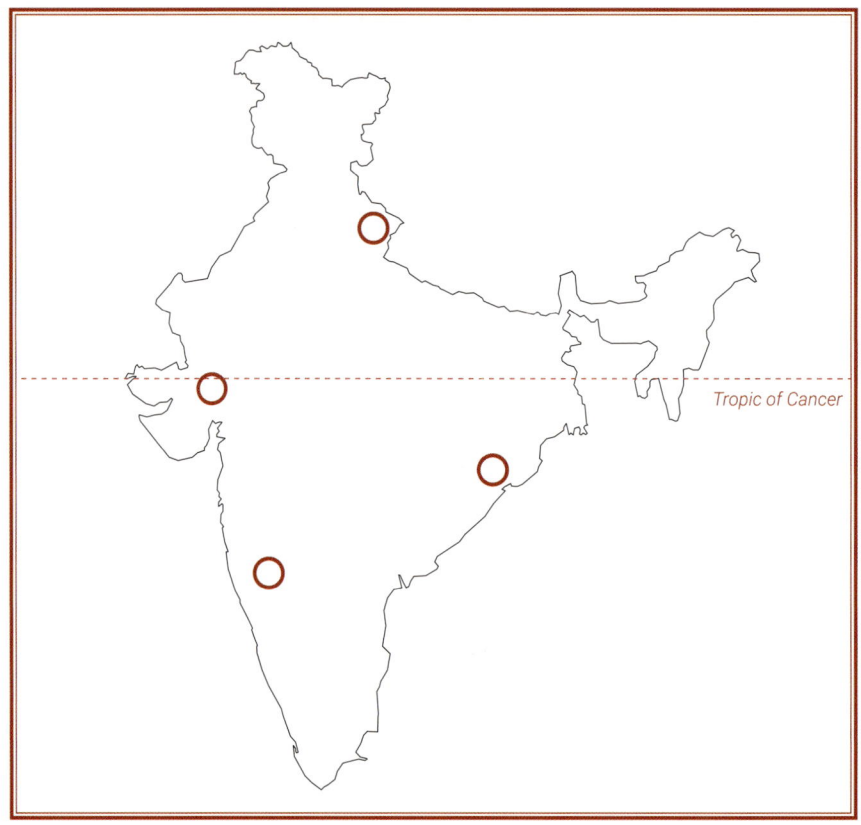

Tropic of Cancer

Activity Three: *Colour—Form and Emptiness*

Stone carvers are very careful about where to leave a space and where to have stone when chiselling a jali design.

In each jali, colour the empty spaces in blue and the stone in brown.

Activity Four: *Complete the Jali-Maze*

Jalis are stone screens carved with intricate geometrical designs. This is a jali from the Sidi Saiyyed Mosque; it is a bush with many branches and flowers entwined around a palm tree.

1) Find your way from the tips of the branches to the main stem of the bush.

2) Draw the missing leaves on the stems, on the left side of the jali.

3) Draw the thick stems. Notice the green dotted line; there are leaves alongside it, but the stems are missing.

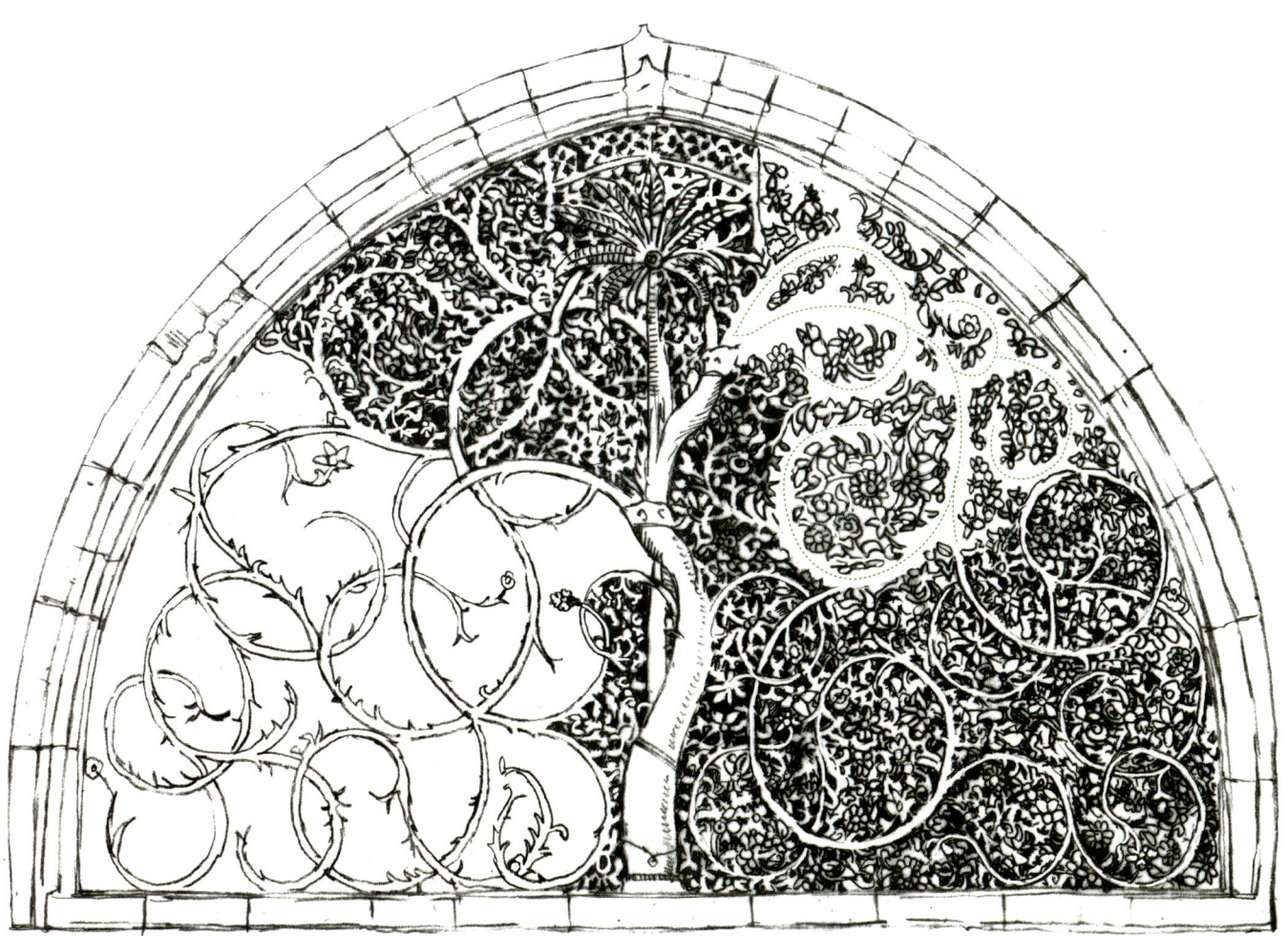

Hill Forts
of Rajasthan

Forts were strongholds where soldiers lived. On all sides, forts had high, stone walls called ramparts and watchtowers from where the warriors kept a lookout for the armies of enemies. Rajasthan has many hill forts. These are built on the tops of hills and in shape, they follow the contour of the hill. Forts always use natural features of the landscape for defence such as the thick forests around Ranthambore Fort, the desert sands surrounding Jaisalmer Fort, and the waters that encircle Gagron Fort.

Narrow trails wind up the hills to these forts of Rajasthan. Many gates called 'pols' have to be crossed before reaching the main centre of the fort. Over time, forts grew bigger and began to have settlements inside them—they even contained entire villages with fields and ponds, as also palaces and temples. Many creative water harvesting methods were

used to collect and preserve water on the hilltops. Merchants and other wealthy people inside the fort lived in breezy multistorey homes with courtyards called havelis. The rulers of Rajasthan were called Rajputs. They loved wrestling, horse riding, camel safaris, elephant rides, and other sports. The Rajputs were also patrons of cultural activities such as art, music, and learning.

Activity One: *Point to Rajasthan*

Left image: Gagron Fort

Below image: Chittorgarh Fort

Activity Two: *Name the Sport and Colour*

Kumbalgarh Fort

Ranthambore Fort

Activity Three: *Play Snakes and Ladders*

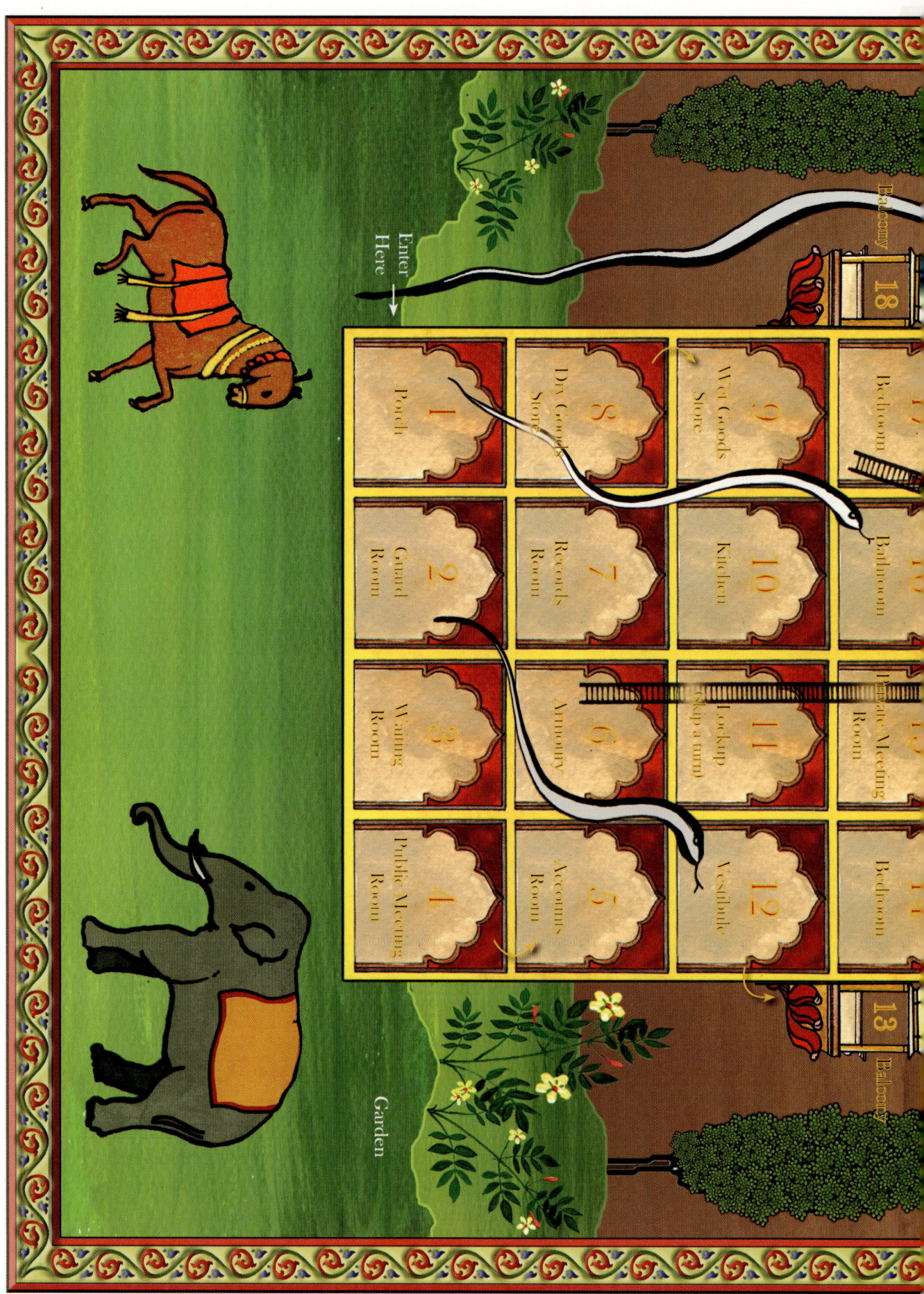

The Agra Fort looks very intimidating from the outside but inside it is a wonderland. To enter it, one had to get past huge bastions or watchtowers, cross over a deep moat full of hungry crocodiles, pass through strong gates studded with spikes, then trudge along outer boundary walls, then along the inner boundary walls—both walls made of huge red sandstone blocks and very high—and finally arrive at the Grand Hall, Diwan-e-Aam. Here the Mughal emperor Shah Jahan would have been seated upon the Peacock Throne hearing the complaints of the common people. In another hall called Diwan-e-Khas, he would have met important people and received special guests. The marble pillars of this hall are breathtaking—colourful floral patterns have been created by inlaying semi-precious stones.

Inside the fort, there is also the beautiful Sheesh Mahal decorated with bits of coloured glass, the lovely pearl-white Moti Masjid, and the Musamman Burj from where the emperor would have enjoyed the breezes cooled by the Yamuna River.

The Agra Fort was earlier known as Badalgarh and used by Rajputs and possibly various sultans. Thereafter it was well cared for by the Mughals. Then, it was seized by the Marathas and eventually by the British, and gradually declined in importance.

Activity One: *Point to Agra*

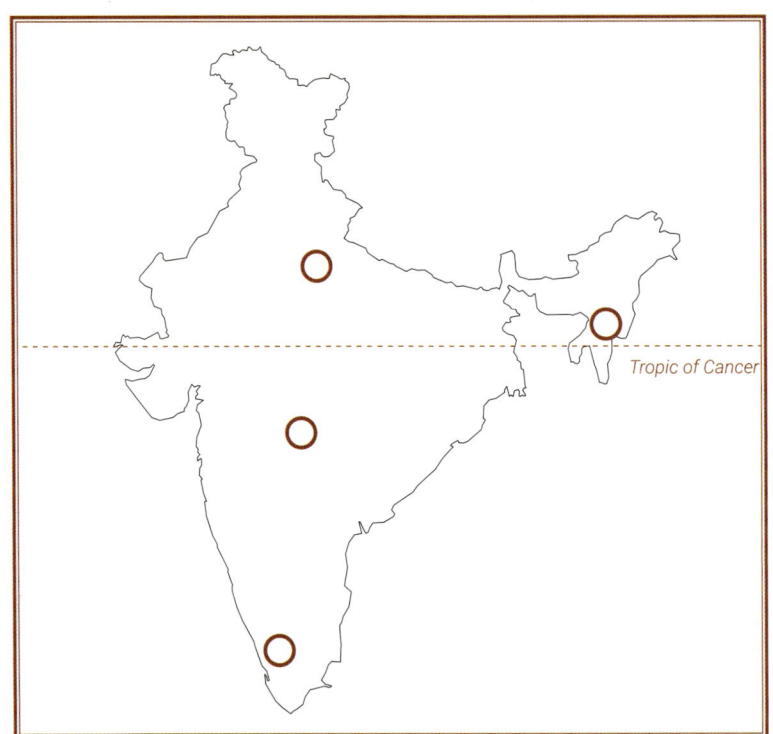

Activity Two: *Identify and Label—Buried History*

Many different people controlled Agra Fort at various points in time. The artefacts below show us the different layers of the past.

1) Plastic comb

2) Chandela statue

3) Sultanate pottery

4) Mineral water bottle

5) Mughal dagger

6) Maratha horseshoe

7) English coin bearing Queen Victoria's portrait

Activity Three: *Colour—The Passing of Shah Jahan: A Painting by Abanindranath Tagore*

The old emperor gazes out at the Taj Mahal on a full moon night from the Musamman Burj where he was put under house arrest by his son Aurangzeb.

Colour by number (Parts of it have been coloured for your reference):

1) Colour 1 as blue
2) Colour 2 as bottle green
3) Colour 3 as red
4) Colour 4 as brown
5) Colour 5 as white/ivory
6) Colour 6 as dark grey
7) Colour 7 as yellow
8) Colour 8 as orange
9) Colour 9 as pink (peach)

Tomb of Humayun in Delhi

Humayun was a famous emperor of the Mughal dynasty, the son of Babur and the father of Emperor Akbar. Humayun is well remembered even after his death, in part, because of a grand monument built over his grave. This sort of a monument is called a tomb or a mausoleum. Moreover, Humayun's magnificent tomb was set in a special garden.

The garden is called char bagh or chahar bagh in Persian, and is designed like the gardens in paradise that are mentioned in the Quran. This garden has four parts that are separated by fountains, pools, and channels of flowing water. Humayun's Tomb was the first garden tomb in India. Later, many copied the idea, including the builder of the Taj Mahal.

Humayun's Tomb is unique for one more reason: it is a storehouse of Mughal graves—about a hundred and fifty family members are also buried here. While the main monument is made of rough sandstone, the graves are often covered with smooth marble. There are arched doors and windows on all sides of the big monument, and on the very top there is a splendid marble dome. Humayun's Tomb looks so beautiful that it could even be a palace.

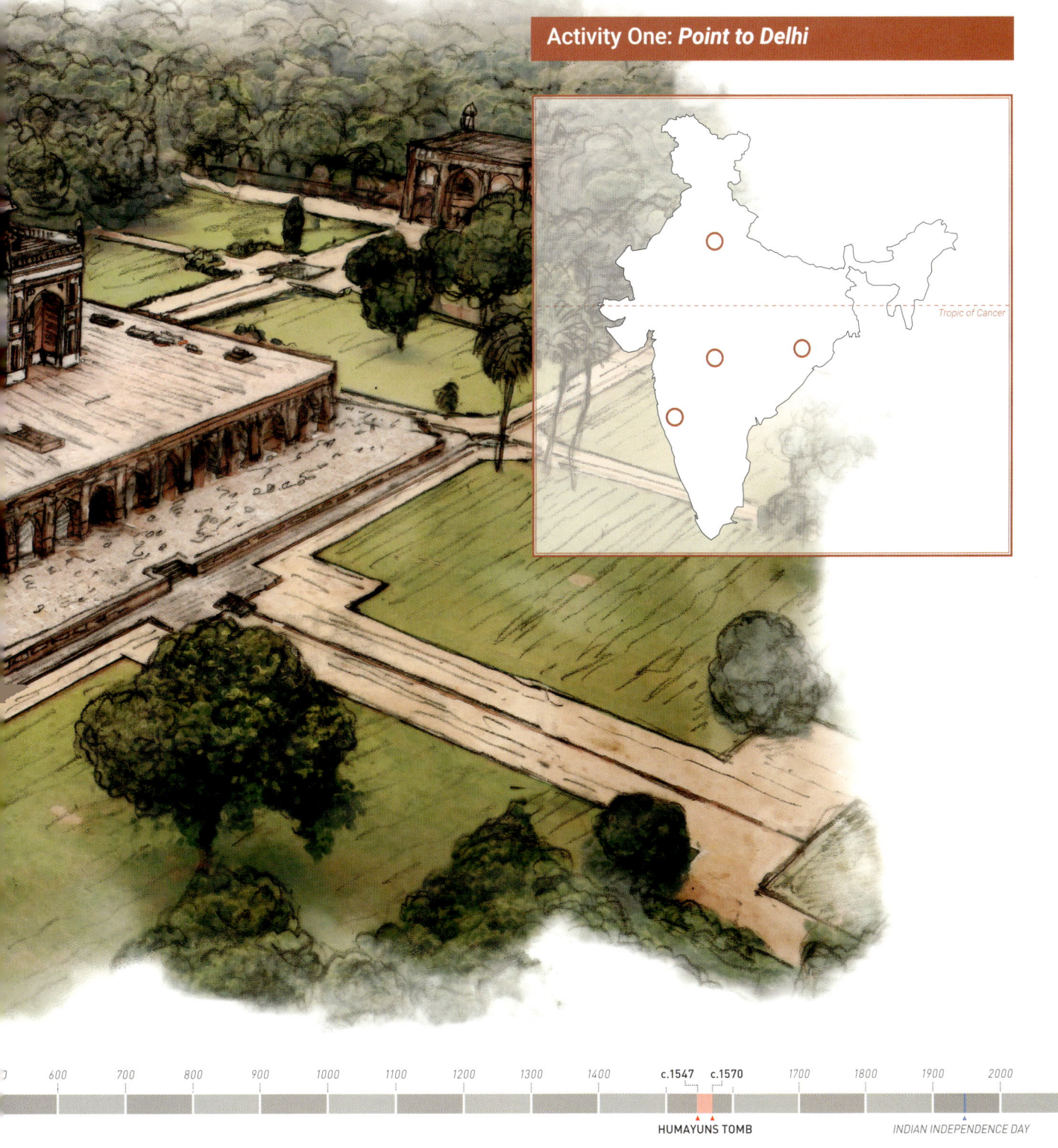

Activity One: *Point to Delhi*

Activity Two: *Label—In Memory of the Dead*

1) **Grave** marks the burial spot of the dead and it is usually covered with a stone slab.

2) **Tomb** or **Mausoleum** is a grand structure built over a grave.

3) **Chattri** is a small pavilion built in memory of a departed person. A chattri symbolizes dignity.

4) **Paliya** is an upright slab of stone that is carved and inscribed, and erected in memory of a deceased hero.

5) **Samadhi Temple** is built in the memory of a saint.

Activity Three: *Colour the Flowers and Birds in a Mughal Garden*

Monuments at Fatehpur Sikri

Fatehpur Sikri was the capital of the grand Mughal empire in the 1570s. Akbar built this 'City of Victory' in the village of Sikri, near Agra. Located close to a gathering place of Sufis, this city welcomed followers of many faiths through its many gates.

The Buland Darwaza at Sikri is the tallest gateway in the world. Immediately beyond lie the Jama Masjid with an enormous courtyard, the tomb of the Sufi saint Salim Chishti, and other religious buildings. Further on, there are private and public halls such as Diwan-e-Khas and Diwan-e-Aam, the royal mint, and the treasury where money was guarded. There are women's palaces with jalis through which ladies could have looked out but not be seen, Akbar's bedroom the Khwabgah, and other palaces and houses.

The royal complex at Fatehpur Sikri also contains areas for leisure and recreation such as the five-storeyed Panch Mahal which is open on all sides, stables for the sure-footed horses and elephants, courtyards for wrestling matches, workshops for crafts, a library, and even a guesthouse for welcoming weary travellers. Additionally, there were sprawling gardens and a pond.

Floral designs, geometric patterns, calligraphy, chattris, and blue glazed tiles that can be seen in Fatehpur show a fusion of styles from different parts of India. Fatehpur was abandoned in the 1580s due to water scarcity. Nonetheless, this city made of red sandstone, is still well preserved.

Activity One: *Point to Fatehpur Sikri*

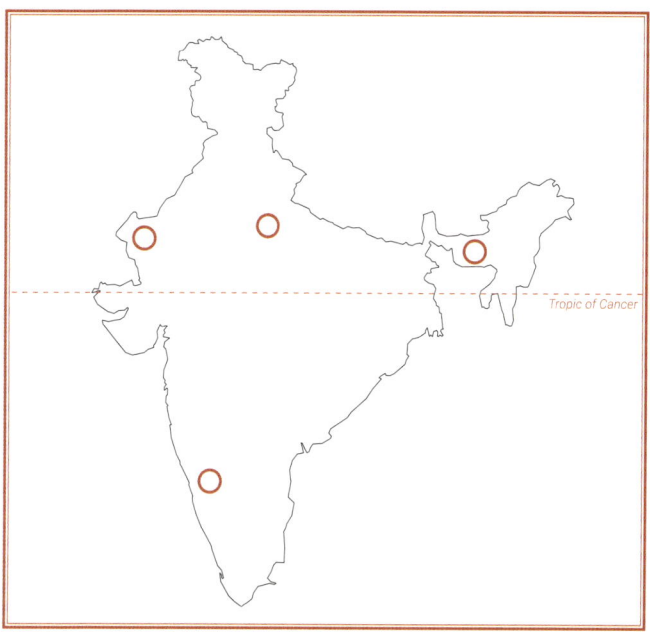

Activity Two: *Identify*

Which three buildings are likely to be breezy and naturally cool in the summer?

Activity Three: *Match the Following*

Group A

1) Akbar founded the religion Din-i-Ilahi

2) Jodha Bai was a Rajput

3) Birbal from the Akbar and Birbal fables was

4) A Sufi saint is an

5) Jama Masjid is a place where

Group B

a) people unite for prayers on Fridays.

b) which was a mixture of many religions.

c) Islamic mystic.

d) princess and a wife of Akbar.

e) a minister and army commander at Akbar's court.

Activity Four: *Multiple Choice*

1) Khwabgah means (*dream palace, fast car, pink phone*).

2) The zenana which is decorated with jalis at Fatehpur Sikri was the residence of (*lions, men, women*).

3) Carawanserai is a (*resting place, electric fan, water pot*) built for (*travellers, caravans, both*).

Activity Five: *Fill in the Blanks*

This is the _____ (*Buland Darwaza, India Gate*) in Fatehpur Sikri. Buland Darwaza means 'Lofty Gate' as well as 'Lofty _____ (*door, drawer*)'. People used to nail _____ (*lamps, horseshoes*) called 'naal' to this wooden door for _____ (*good luck, bad luck*).

Activity Six: *Look and Answer—Mihrab*

Look at this mihrab in the Jama Masjid at Fatehpur Sikri.

1) Fill in the Blanks:

A mihrab resembles a _____ (*nose, niche*) in a wall of a mosque. The mihrab tells us where _____ (*Mecca, Mexico*), the holy place for Muslims, is located. In India, the mihrab always points to the _____ (*west, bakery*), which is the direction of prayer. A mihrab is painstakingly decorated with _____ (*patterns, tumblers*). A mihrab also _____ (*amplifies, paints*) the sound of prayers offered in the mosque.

2) Label:

a) floral motifs   b) stars   c) carvings   d) calligraphy   e) geometric motifs

Activity Seven: *Label the Coins*

In addition to commissioned books, paintings, and buildings, Akbar had exquisite coins minted. The coins were of different shapes, sizes, and metals. Here are several coins with both sides shown.

1) Daam, a small round copper coin

2) Rupee, a round silver coin

3) Mohur, a round gold coin with a duck

4) Mehrabi, a gold coin shaped like a mihrab

5) Daam, a square copper coin

6) Rupee, a square silver coin

7) Mohur, a square gold coin

The Red Fort at Delhi

The Red Fort has three stories to tell.

The first is about the Mughal rulers, their power, wealth, and style. Shah Jahan shifted the Mughal capital to Delhi, along with his Peacock Throne, and there he built a fort mightier than the Agra Fort. This new fort, called the Red Fort, also contained palaces, gardens, mosques, halls; and here too, older Indian designs were combined with newer Persian ones. Each space was as charming as its name: Nahr-i-Behisht (Stream of Paradise) was located in the garden, Chhatta Chowk was a market inside the fort where luxurious items were sold, Rang Mahal was a lively palace, and so on. The Yamuna River used to flow along the front of the fort. Behind the fort there were the homes of common folk, their market and mosque.

The second story is about modern India, her strength and independence. On 15 August 1947, Jawaharlal Nehru unfurled India's flag from the ramparts of the Red Fort. Since then, every year on Independence Day, the prime minister hoists the national flag from the same place.

There is a third story too: of loot and plunder. As the force of the Mughals weakened, the colonial rulers wrecked the place, followed by many others. They greedily pulled out silver from the ceilings, pried out precious and semi-precious stones from their grand settings, and also took away furniture and other valuable items. The legend of the bejewelled Peacock Throne tells us that it was robbed and taken apart in Iran. Now, the Archaeological Survey of India protects this historic site.

Activity One: *Colour the Red Fort*

Activity Two: *Label*

Notice the people and activities outside the walls of the Red Fort.

1) Dancer

2) Account keeper

3) Artist

4) Blind musician

5) Merchant

6) Sufi-fakir

Activity Three: *Point to Delhi*

Activity Four: *Join the Dots and Label*

Weapons of the Mughal Era: **Battleaxe, Dagger, Knife, Sword, Shield, Mace,** and **Musket**.

Activity Five: *Match the Following—Buildings of the Red Fort*

Group A

1) Hamam

2) Baoli

3) Hayat Bakhsh Bagh

4) Moti Masjid

Group B

a) is the stepwell that provided fresh water.

b) is the royal bathhouse.

c) is a pretty mosque.

d) is a charming garden.

Activity Six: *Fill in the Blanks*

1) The Red Fort or Lal Qila is named thus because it is made of _____ (*red sandstone, white marble*).

2) The Lahore Gate and the Delhi Gate are the famous _____ (*entry and exit points, ponds and lakes*).

3) Naubat Khana is where _____ (*drums were beaten, carpets were beaten*) to announce the arrival of important people.

4) Diwan-e-Khas and Diwan-e-Aam were the _____ (*audience halls, bedrooms*) where special and common people came to meet the emperor.

5) Hira Mahal, Khas Mahal, Mumtaz Mahal, and Rang Mahal are the names of _____ (*palaces, hotels*) where the emperor and his relatives resided.

Taj Mahal

The first sight of the Taj Mahal makes everybody gasp, it is splendid! What makes the Taj so extraordinary? There are some obvious reasons such as the white, polished marble that glows; the love story of Shah Jahan who built this in memory of his favourite wife, Mumtaz; the inlay work on the walls that is as fine as jewellery work; the marble screens that create patterns of light and shadows; the pool of water that reflects the monument on moonlit nights.

Then, there are details that experts such as artists and architects might notice. Different shapes have been skillfully blended such as domes, arches, spires, vertical minarets, rectangular doorways, and octagonal rooms. There are also elements that are

at Agra

purposely positioned at different heights, depths, and distances to create special effects. For example: the Taj is built upon a platform and from a distance, it appears to be floating; Quranic verses that are etched at a great height are larger in size than others so as not to look distorted when seen from below.

It is not hard to believe that thousands of human workers were needed to create this monument, as were hundreds of elephants to haul marble, miles of ramps to move the construction material, twenty-eight types of precious and semi-precious stones from India and from foreign lands, millions of rupees, and nearly twenty years.

Activity One: *Point to Agra*

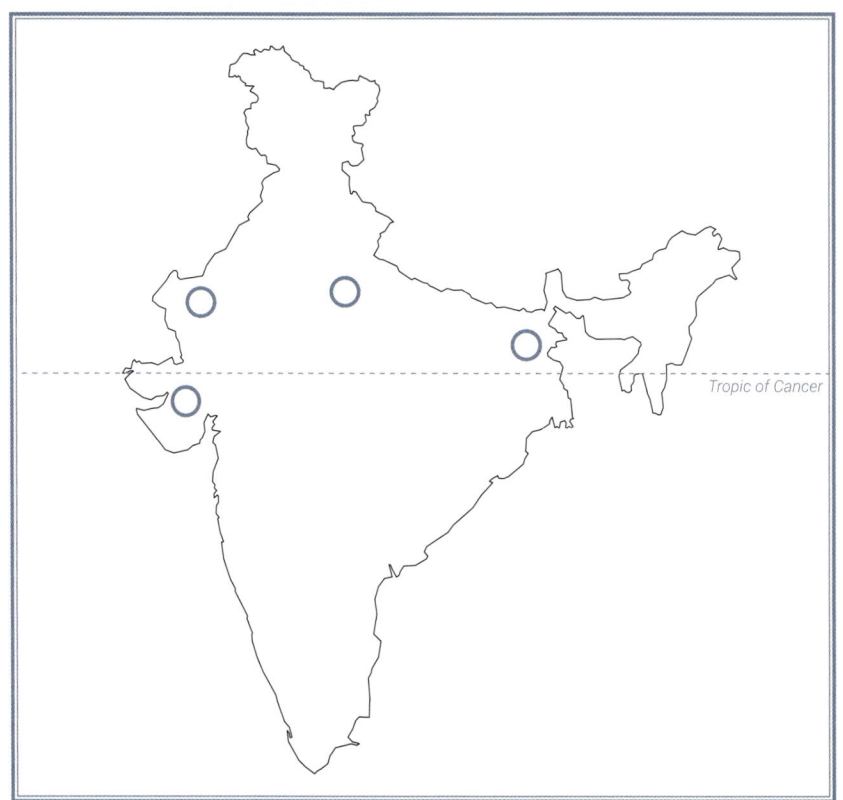

Activity Two: *Colour (Right)*

Precious and semi-precious stones have been embedded into the marble, this is called inlay work.

Activity Three: *Cross out the Wrong Words*

The following experts were needed for constructing the Taj Mahal:

Masons, Stone cutters, Inlayers, Carvers, Painters, Calligraphers, Dome builders, Horticulture planners, Architects, Cooks, Drivers, Dancers, Cowherds, Singers, Doctors, Priests

Activity Four: Label

Notice the features (also called elements) of the Taj Mahal:

1) Finial (Tip)   2) Dome   3) Arches   4) Chattris   5) Minarets   6) Platform (base)

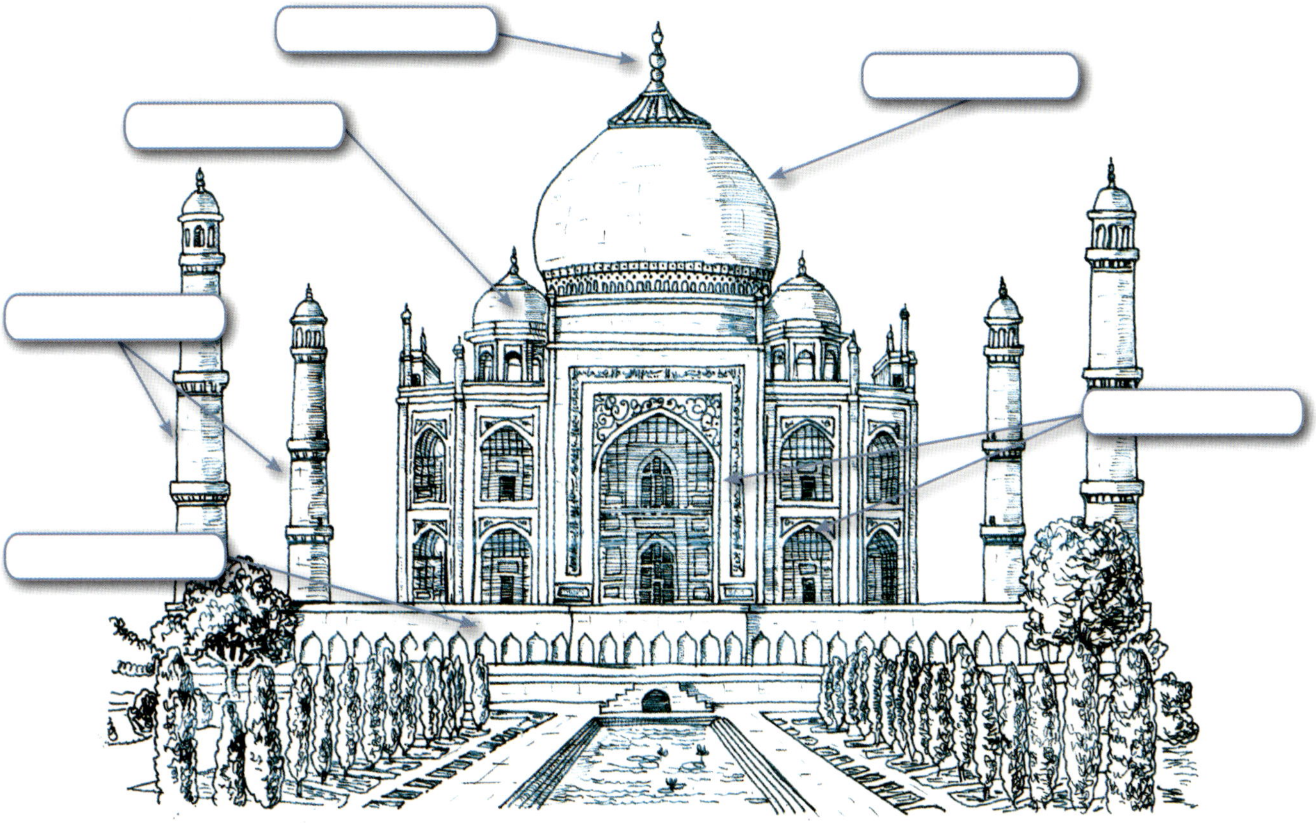

Activity Five: Draw the Taj Mahal—Bilateral Symmetry

Notice how the left and the right sides are the same.

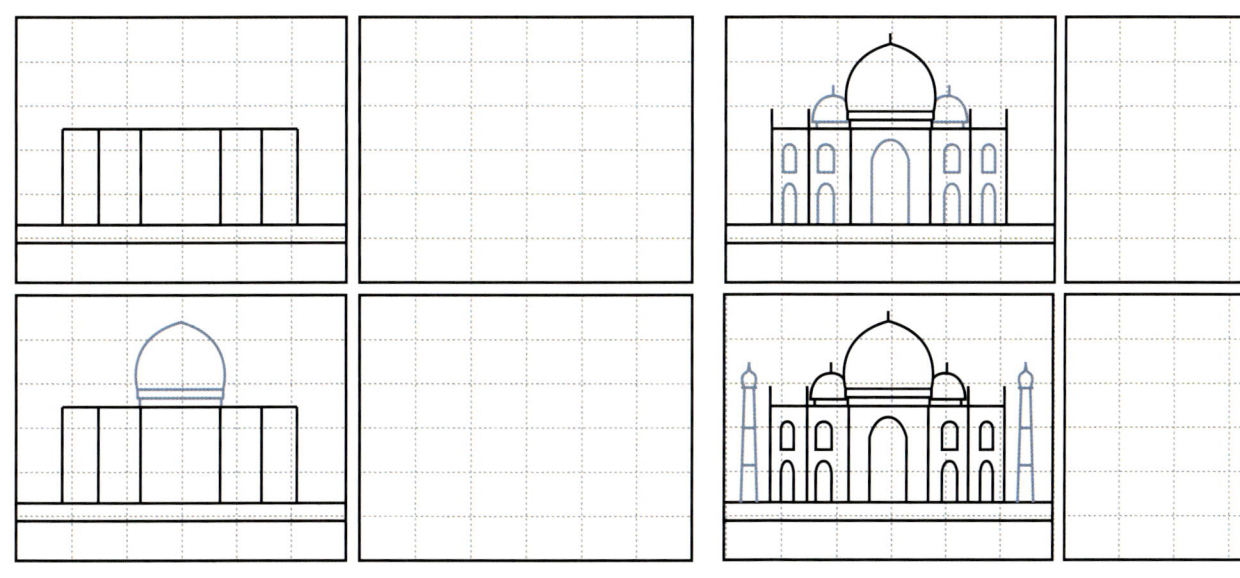

Activity Six: *Pick the Correct Answer*

Many people tried to copy the famous Taj Mahal at Agra, but their final results were not the same.

1) A Dutch soldier wanted the tomb over his grave to look like the Taj Mahal, however it looks odd because:

a) the material is largely red sandstone.
b) it looks like a car.
c) it looks like a Chola Temple.

Tomb of a Dutchman, Agra, India

Pandal at Durga Puja, Kolkata, India

2) A group of people made a Durga Puja pandal near Kolkata that looked like the Taj Mahal, however it is different because:

a) it was built to last only for a few days, i.e. temporary.
b) it was green in colour.
c) it had a gopuram.

3) In Sonargaon, Bangladesh they tried to make a copy of the Taj Mahal, however it looks different because:

a) it does not have fountains.
b) it does not have minarets.
c) the size and ratio of the various parts are not the same as the Agra Taj.

Monument at Sonargaon, Bangladesh

4) The Brighton Royal Pavilion, a palace in England, attempted to copy the beauty of the Taj Mahal, however it looks bizarre because:

a) it is a muddle of styles and features.
b) it looks like an airplane.
c) it looks like a stepwell.

Royal Pavilion England

Trump Resort and Casino, USA

5) A gambling house in New Jersey was named Taj Mahal and was made to look like the Taj, however it is very odd because:

a) it does not have a dome.
b) it does not have a fountain.
c) it is not for the purpose of preserving the memory of a beloved wife.

6) A copy of the Taj Mahal has been made in Aurangabad, however it looks different because:

a) it is set within a garden.
b) the proportions are different (i.e. too tall and too narrow).
c) it has arches.

Bibi Ka Maqbara, Aurangabad, India

Mahabat Maqbara, Junagarh, India

7) At Junagarh too, they have tried to copy the Taj Mahal however it looks different because:

a) it is raised up high on a grand platform.
b) some winding steps have been added.
c) it is made using shining white marble.

Churches and Convents
of Goa

In Goa, white churches stand out against a blue sea and palm trees. Until recently, Goa was a colony of Portugal. With great zeal, the Portuguese established their faith in this land. They replicated the architectural style and traditions of the famous churches of Europe. UNESCO felt that this was a very unique transportation of culture and needed to be noticed by the whole world. Hence, seven churches and convents were chosen for special care and attention. Convents were cloistered spaces strictly meant for nuns, women who spent their lives in the service of god, while churches were used by all genders of worshippers and generally managed by monks and priests.

The Church of St Augustine lies in total ruins and is a silent, mysterious place; it makes us think about the journeys, missions, and difficulties faced by the Christian groups in India. Meanwhile, many churches of Goa are intact with lovely altar pieces, wonderful wooden statuettes, and historic paintings.

However, the greatest wonder is at the Basilica of Bom Jesus, where the 500-year-old embalmed remains of St Francis Xavier are preserved in a glass casket.

Activity One: *Label the Churches*

1) Church of Our Lady Rosary

2) Se Cathedral

3) Church of Saint Augustine

4) Church and Convent of Saint Francis of Assisi

5) Chapel of Saint Catherine

6) Basilica of Bom Jesus

7) Church of Saint Cajetan

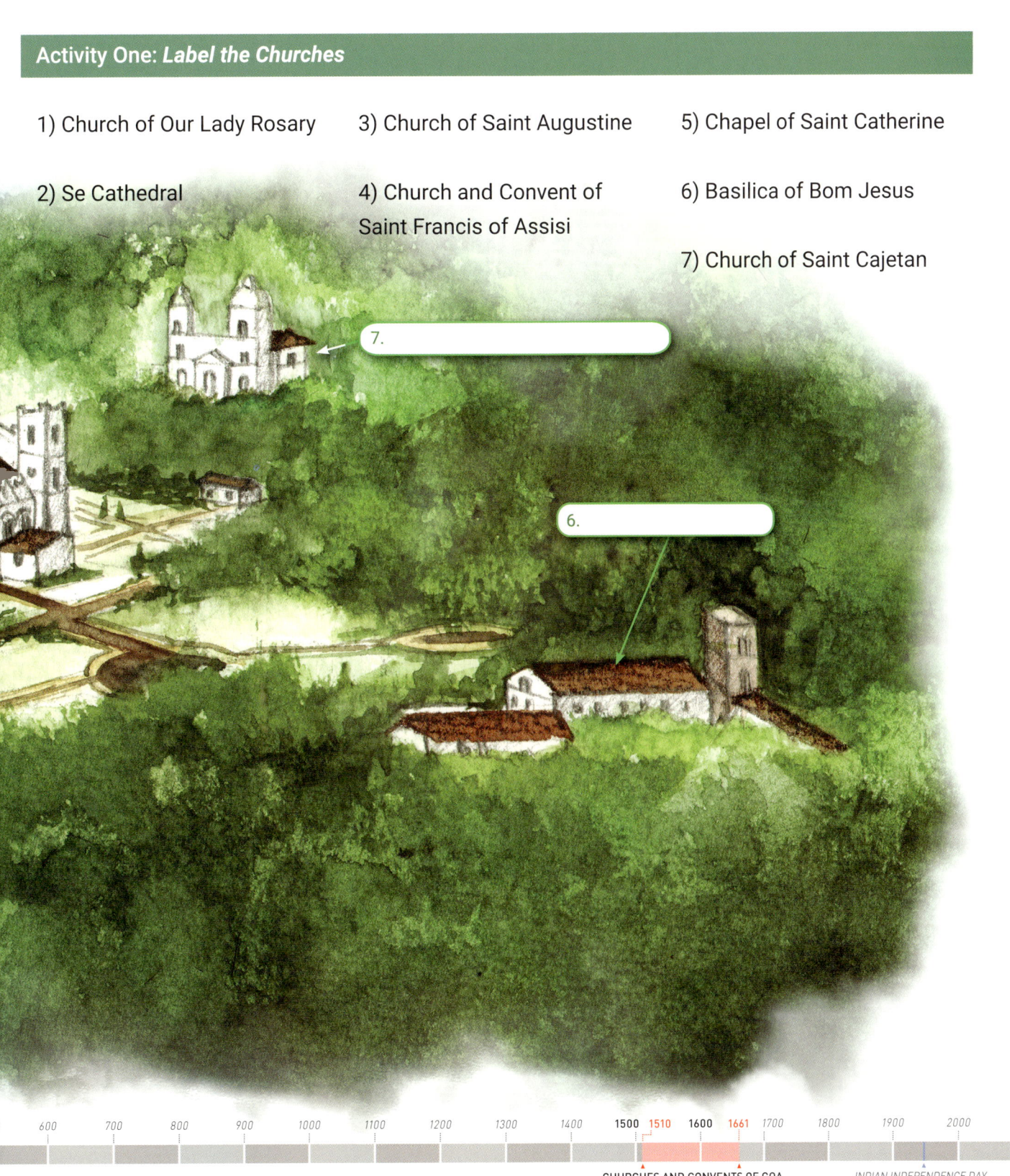

Activity Two: *Point to Goa and Portugal*

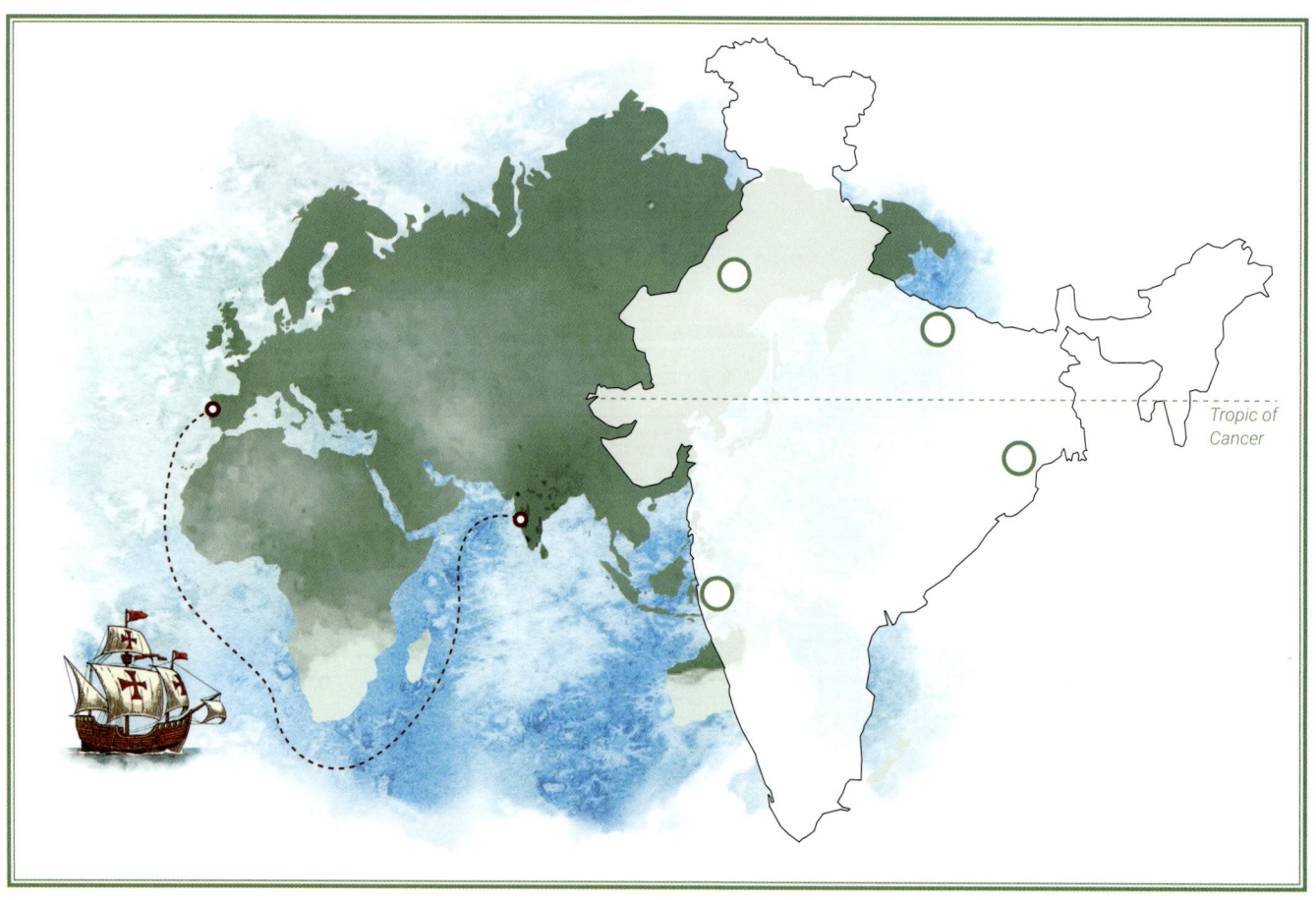

Activity Three: *Find the Names—Christian Groups*

1) Catholic

2) Jesuit

3) Franciscan

4) Carmelite

5) Dominican

X	X	X	X	J	E	S	U	I	T
X	X	X	X	X	X	X	X	X	X
C	A	R	M	E	L	I	T	E	X
Y	Y	Y	Y	Y	Y	Y	Y	Y	Y
Y	D	O	M	I	N	I	C	A	N
Y	Y	Y	Y	Y	Y	Z	Z	Z	Z
F	R	A	N	C	I	S	C	A	N
Z	Z	Z	Z	Z	Z	Z	Z	Z	Z
Z	Z	C	A	T	H	O	L	I	C

Activity Four: *Colour the Two Wooden Statuettes*

Use red, yellow, brown, green, and blue

Mother Mary holding Jesus

Saint Francis of Assisi

Activity Five: *Draw a Bell Tower and a Cross*

The Bell Tower on the left side of Se Cathedral collapsed; it was exactly like the one on the right.

1) Draw the missing bell tower.

2) Then, draw a bell inside the bell tower.

3) Now draw a cross in the centre of the church, i.e., on top of the triangular portion.

143

Jaipur City in Rajasthan

Most cities in our country have grown naturally. They were not rigidly planned cities. Jaipur however, was a completely new city born in the eighteenth century, designed carefully by Maharaja Sawai Jai Singh.

Jaipur was laid out as a grid. The streets meet at intersections called chaupars. These chaupars were large public squares and used to have water reservoirs when the city was first built. Moreover, Jaipur was envisioned as a trade city. The maharaja wished for the city to have many crafts and industries. Thus each neighbourhood, called chowkri, specialized in one craft—lacquerware, jewellery, painting, pottery, and so on.

Activity One: *Point to Jaipur*

Activity Two: *Draw*

Draw two faces peering out of the jharokas.

Today, as before, the streets of the old city are lined with shops that are situated in red sandstone buildings with tall, thick, round columns. The fronts of these buildings have grand entrances and pretty balconies called jharokas.

Jaipur has many temples such as Govinda Dev, and also elegant monuments such as the Hawa Mahal (Palace of Winds), the Isarlat Sargasuli (Tower to Heaven), the Jantar Mantar (the giant observatory), and the Jaipur City Palace. The novelty of the city plan and the different cultures and idioms that influenced it make it a unique city.

| 600 | 700 | 800 | 900 | 1000 | 1100 | 1200 | 1300 | 1400 | 1500 | 1600 | Founded 1727 | 1800 | 1900 | 2000 |

JAIPUR CITY   INDIAN INDEPENDENCE DAY

Activity Three: *Discover Jaipur—Map Reading*

1) Fill in the Blanks

a) There are roughly _____ (*three, nine*) squares in the grid.

b) The old city has _____ (*eight, two*) gates.

c) The road from _____ (*Suraj Pol, Amer Pol*) to _____ (*Kishan Pol, Chand Pol*) goes in an east-west direction, similar to the movement of the sun and the moon.

d) The above-mentioned road passes through _____ (*three, ten*) chaupars, and the _____ (*Tripolia, Motikatla*) Bazaar.

e) The most important buildings such as the _____ (*City Palace, fruit shop*) and the _____ (*Govind Dev Temple, City Gate*) are located near the town centre.

Index

- Gates
- Monuments
- Squares
- Market
- Localities

2) Draw, with a blue pen, the route from Amer Pol to Chand Pol and...

3) Circle three places that the above route will not pass through

Hawa Mahal

Ramganj Chaupar

Jantar Mantar

Isarlat Sargasuli

Kishan Pol

Surasti Pur

Badi Chaupar

Chhoti Chaupar

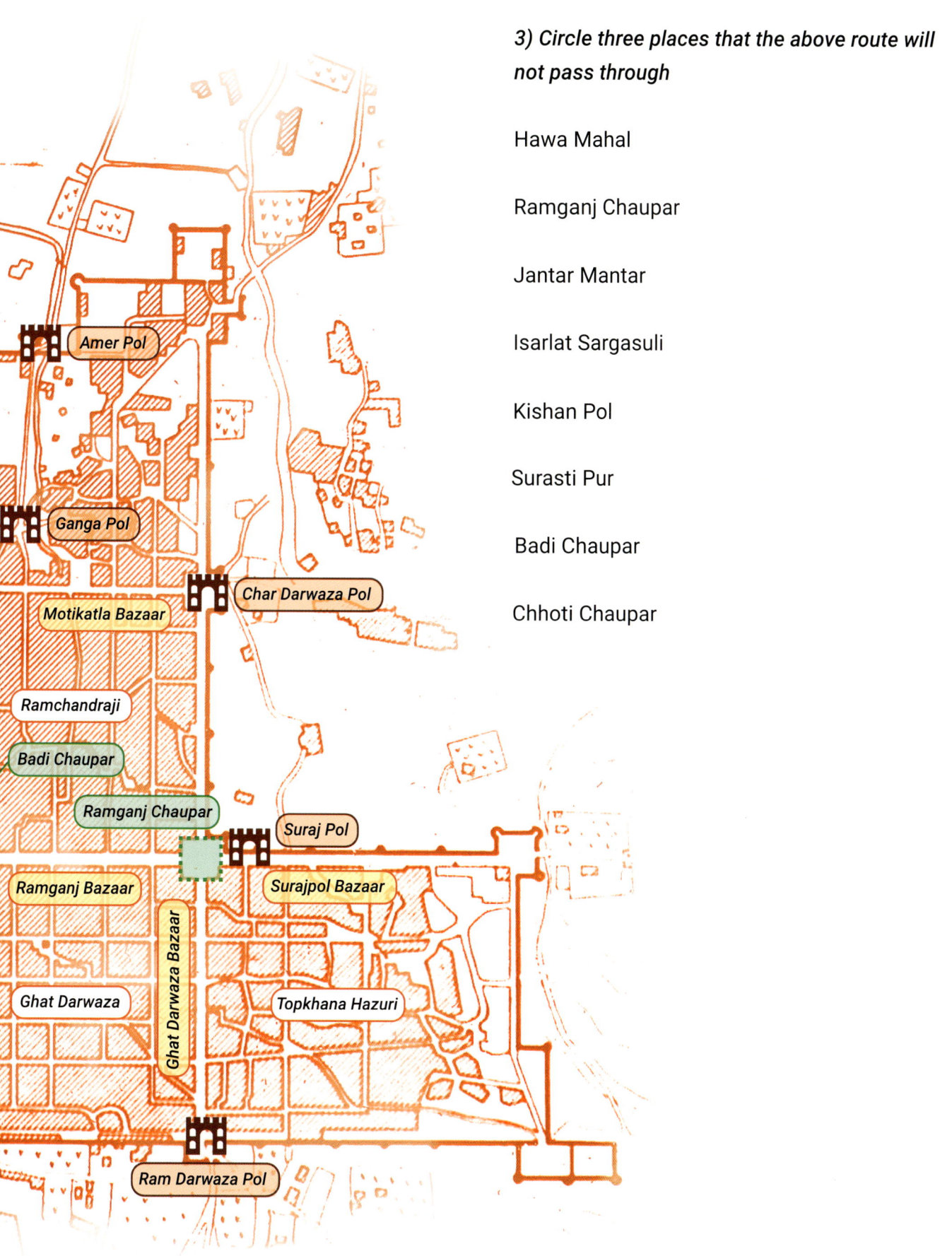

Activity Four: *Match—Textile Designs*

Brightly coloured fabrics with colourful motifs were printed in Jaipur using carved wooden blocks.

1) Singh Baaj (Lion's claw)
2) Ankhada (Nose ring)
3) Mirchi (Chilli)
4) Chhota phool (Small flower)
3) Kharbhuja (Watermelon)
6) Jali (Screen)

Activity Five: *Printing*

Just like wooden blocks, vegetables too can be used to make prints.

Follow these steps to create patterns in the space provided.

Step 1: *Take a bhindi (okra) and cut it into half.*

Step 2: *Dip the bhindi into the paint.*

Step 3: *Stamp the painted side of the bhindi on the space provided.*

Jantar Mantar at Jaipur

Before the invention of mechanical and digital clocks and of huge telescopes, people had very different ways of telling time and of studying the skies. Jai Singh was a king who was very interested in calculating time and also in knowing the positions of the planets and stars. In the 1700s, he built an observatory complex in Jaipur called Jantar Mantar. There are approximately twenty fixed instruments in this complex, such as the Dhruva Darshak Pattika, which finds the location of the pole star, and the Samrat Yantra, which measures time using shadows.

Activity One: *Point to Jaipur*

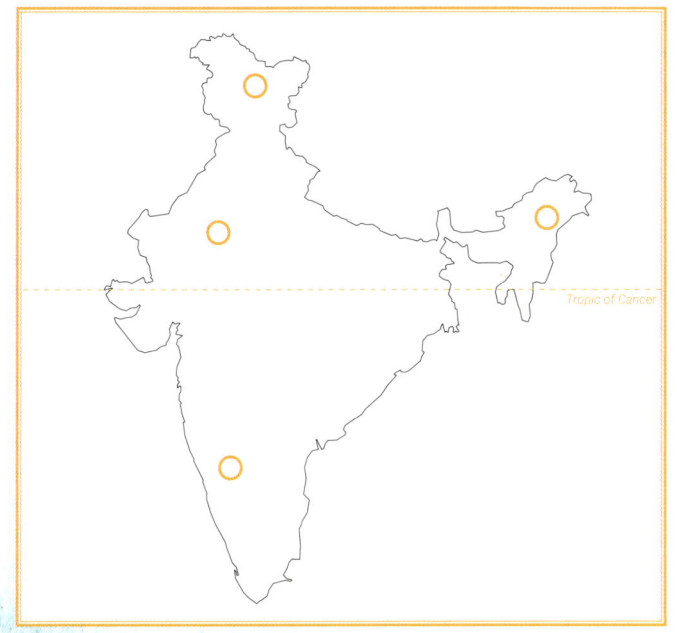

Astronomers, experts who studied the position of the sun and other celestial objects, would make very accurate observations every day, and these would be used in creating calendars for different communities. Lunar and solar eclipses, fasting and feasting days were predicted.

The Jantar Mantar gets its name from yantra meaning instruments and mantrana meaning to calculate. It is one of the largest and best-preserved observatories in India, and it was built based on astronomy traditions learnt from many parts of the world. It made experts and ordinary people think rationally; to think about the idea of time-telling as an everyday act in an era when this was not common.

Activity Two: *Draw*

Where will the shadow of the pot fall at sunset?

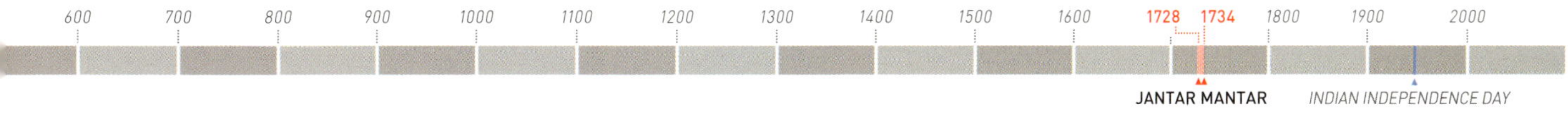

| 600 | 700 | 800 | 900 | 1000 | 1100 | 1200 | 1300 | 1400 | 1500 | 1600 | 1728 | 1734 | 1800 | 1900 | 2000 |

JANTAR MANTAR   INDIAN INDEPENDENCE DAY

Activity Three: *Calendar*

The outer perimeter of this Rajput calendar depicts the nine planetary deities. The inner perimeter depicts the twelve zodiac signs.

1) Write the name of the current month and year.

2) Fill in all the dates of the current month.

3) Circle your zodiac sign.

Activity Four: *Identify the Seasons*

In Jaipur, a set of twelve miniature paintings were produced called the Baramasa Paintings; they represent the twelve months of the year.

1) A spring scene with a Holi fire.

2) A summer scene with sunny skies and a fruiting tree.

3) A monsoon scene with clouds and rain.

4) A winter scene with Diwali oil lamps and dark starry skies.

Victorian Gothic and Art Deco
at Mumbai

The densely populated city of Mumbai on the west coast of India has the second largest collection of art deco buildings in the world, as well as some of the best examples of Victorian Neo-Gothic buildings. Both these styles originated in Europe but Mumbai, which was a sea port, and already a major trading city and a governmental hub, decided to adopt these as it pushed to become a more modern and stylish city.

The art deco buildings are primarily residential such as the Soona Mahal and the Motabhoy Mansion. There are also cinema halls such as the Regal and the Liberty. These art deco buildings were inspired by new technologies and were made of steel columns and concrete beams instead

of brick and stone. Their sleek designs were influenced by aeroplanes, automobiles, and especially ocean liners. Art deco buildings can often be recognized by their grills and railings that might have reminders of the sea or by the frozen fountain motif.

The Gothic style buildings are older and are primarily public buildings such as the university campus and the High Court. A few Indian touches were often added to these such as balconies, verandas, or ideas from palaces. Thereby, a new style developed that can be called Indo-Gothic and Indo-deco.

Activity One: *Point to Mumbai*

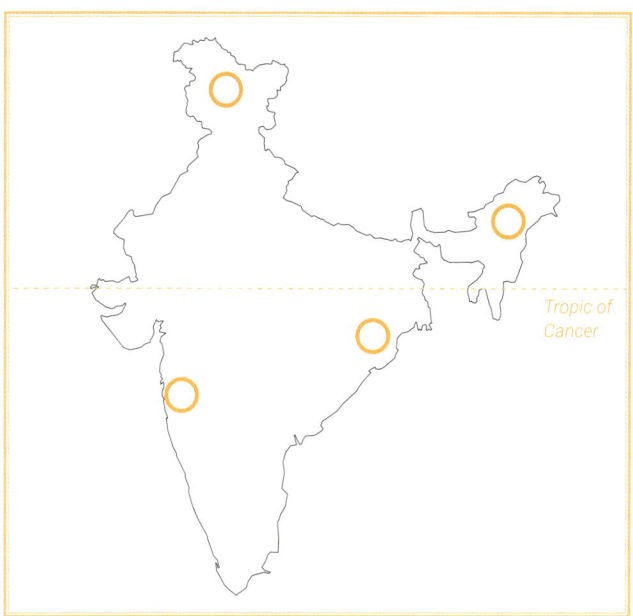

Tropic of Cancer

Activity Two: *Colour*

Stained-glass windows are a typical feature of Gothic buildings. This window is in the Rajabai Clock Tower of Mumbai University.

Parts of the glass window have been coloured in. Use that as a guide to fill in the rest with the following colours:

- Red
- Light Green
- Maroon
- Blue
- Orange
- Dark Green
- Yellow

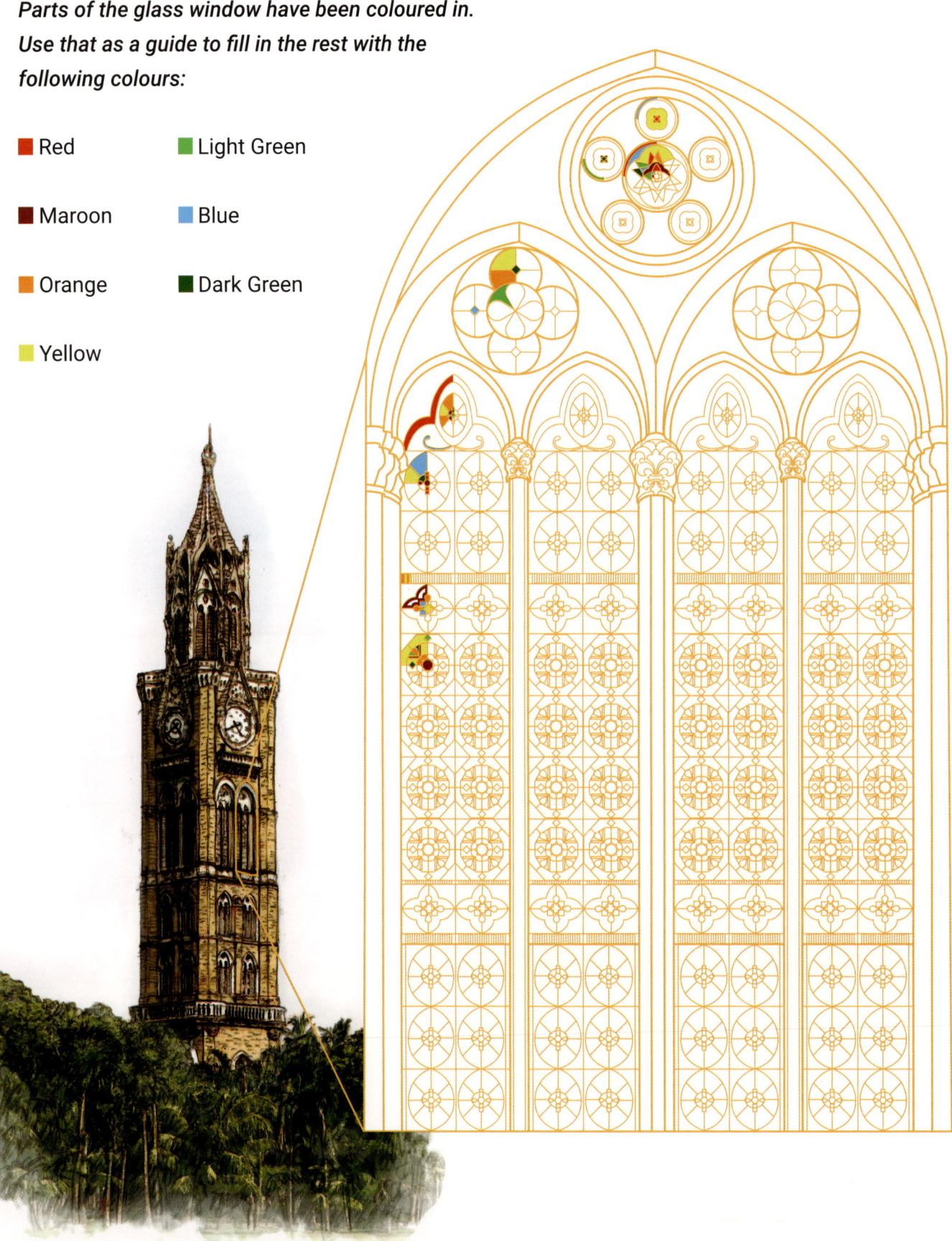

Activity Three: *Tick the Correct Statements*

Compare the Soona Mahal building overlooking the Arabian Sea and the ship.

1) Both have curving lines of small windows

2) Both are enormous

3) Both puff out smoke from the smokestack

4) Both are of a similar shape

5) Both can float on water

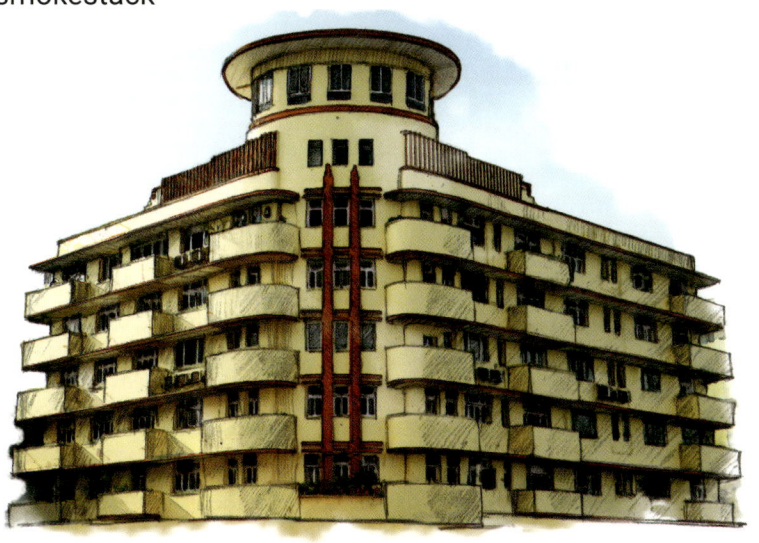

Activity Four: *Draw a Window, a Grill, and a Railing*

1) This is a window shaped like a porthole. The wavy line indicates the sea and in the centre there is a palm tree. **Draw one more such window.**

2) This motif on a railing represents a frozen fountain. **Draw one more such motif.**

3) This is a grill. The wavy lines indicate the sea, the curls are waves, and the circle represents the setting sun. **Draw one more such grill.**

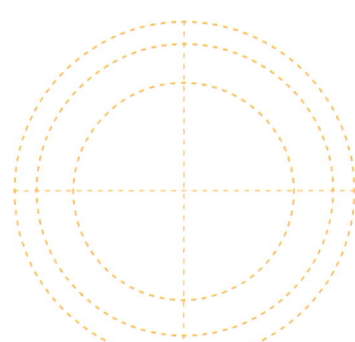

Chhatrapati Shivaji Terminus at Mumbai

The Chhatrapati Shivaji Terminus is one of the grandest railway stations in the world. A British architect, F. W. Stevens, worked with Indian craftspersons to create a station like none other.

It is huge and busy of course; what is surprising however are the numerous delicate features such as rose windows with stained glass, carvings of dancing peacocks, flowers and vines, stone mesh work, and so on. It is unique because it also gracefully combines ideas from separate cultures, that is Victorian Italianate Gothic Revival Architecture and Indian palaces.

The entrance to the Chhatrapati Shivaji Terminus makes the first statement. One column is crowned with a seated lion representing the United Kingdom, and another with a crouching tiger representing India.

The material used ranges from the local yellow malad stone, to Italian marble, to teak wood from Burma. Further, there are sculpted faces of different castes and communities of India. There are also faces of ten past directors of the Great Indian Peninsula Railway Company (GIPR) staring at the commuters.

There are gargoyles jutting out of the walls and carvings of monkeys scampering amongst foliage, mongooses, and cobras. There are arches, domes, and turrets, all finely blended to form this magnificent railway terminus.

Activity One: *Point to Mumbai*

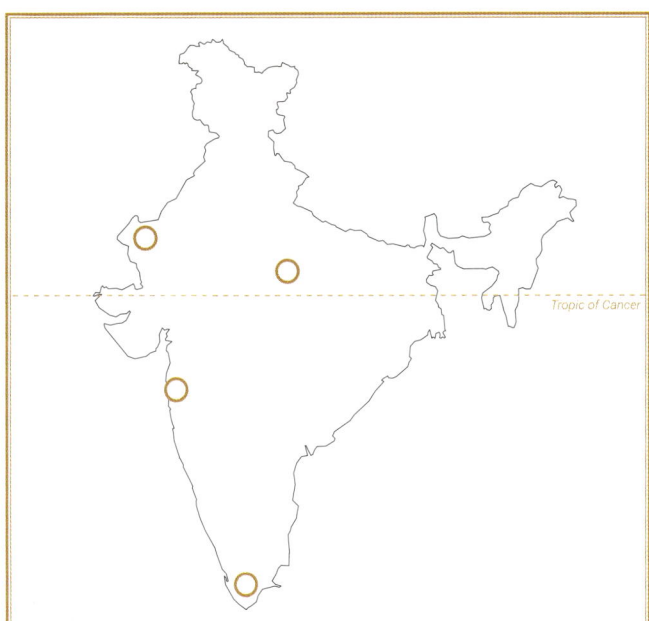

Activity Two: *Label the Following*

1) Dome
2) Pointed turrets
3) Rose window
4) Stained glass
5) Round arches
6) Pointed arches
7) Gargoyles jutting out of walls

Activity Three: *Match the Following*

1) Dancing peacock

2) Flowers and leaves

3) Stone mesh work (jali work)

4) Mongoose

5) Monkey

6) Cobra

7) Faces of people of different castes and communities of India

8) Roundels with past directors of the railways

9) Gargoyle

Le Corbusier's Capitol Complex at Chandigarh

The Capitol Complex at Chandigarh is a set of buildings and monuments designed by Le Corbusier in the 1950s, shortly after the independence of India. Le Corbusier was a French–Swiss architect. He designed many buildings around the world using columns, slabs, and steps. UNESCO appreciated his effort to understand the needs of human beings and his desire to create an architectural style that could be used by millions to build inexpensive houses anywhere. Therefore, seventeen complexes that Le Corbusier built, spread over seven continents, were given the special status of 'World Heritage Site'.

Corbusier's monuments and buildings in Chandigarh mark a high point in an architectural movement called the International Modern Style. At the Capitol Complex, there are three administrative buildings: Legislative Assembly, Secretariat, and High Court; and four other monuments: Open Hand Monument, Tower of Shadows, Geometric Hill, and Martyrs Monument. There is also a lake.

The Capitol Complex was planned with wide roads and roundabouts so that traffic could flow smoothly. The concrete buildings remain naturally cool—sunscreens and pools help in this regard. Le Corbusier also used many different signs and symbols in the structures that he designed.

Activity Two: *Draw a Building—Le Corbusier's Modular Architecture*

Add two storeys to this building by drawing columns, then slabs, and finally steps.

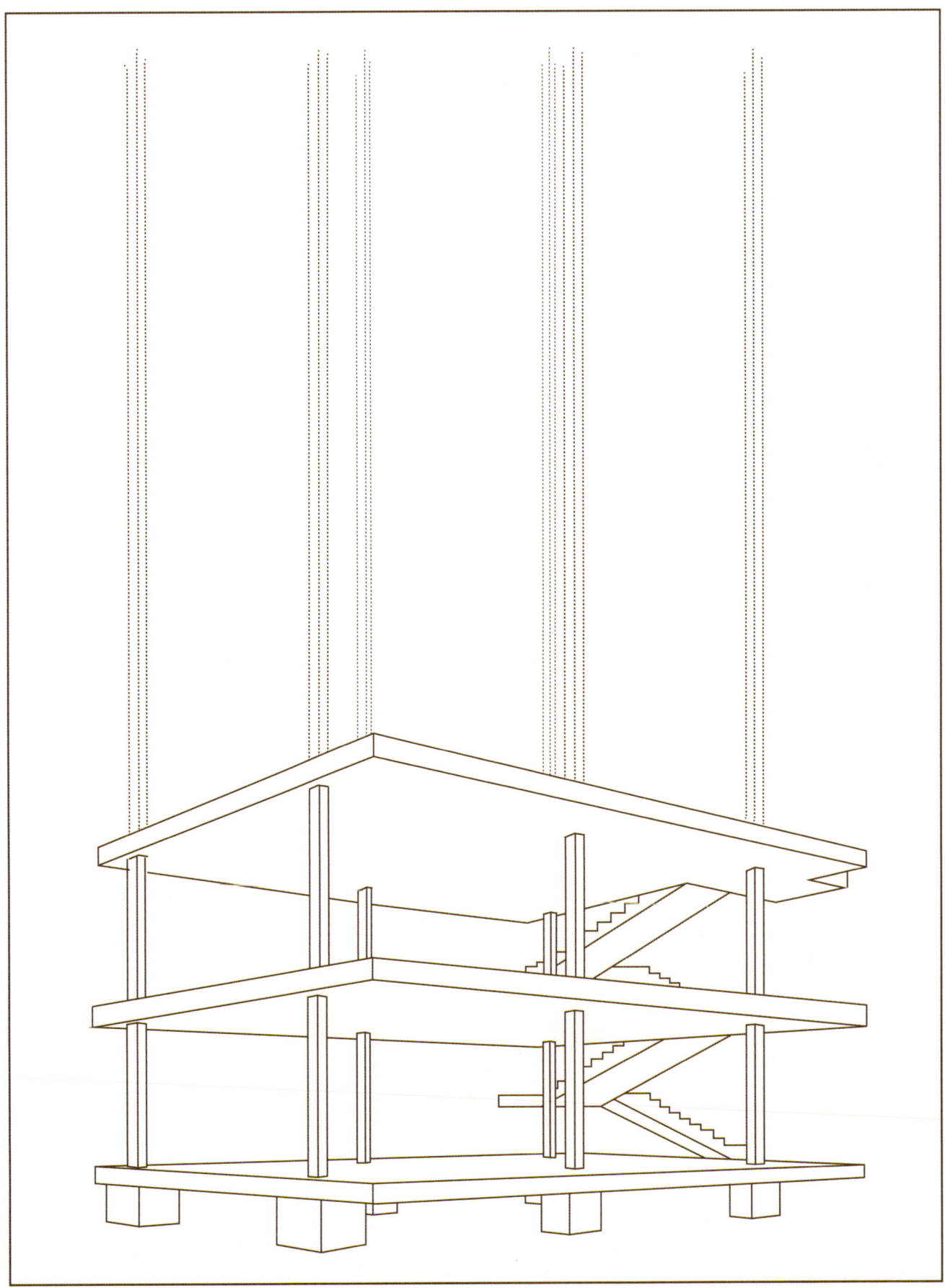

Activity Three: *Draw the Open Hand Monument*

Put your own hand on this page and draw the outline of your hand. Then draw a base for it, like at Chandigarh. Then turn your hand-drawing into a bird (with an eye, beak, feathers) and colour.